The Leap of Reason

BOOKS BY DON CUPITT
Published by The Westminster Press

The Leap of Reason
Crisis of Moral Authority
Christ and the Hiddenness of God

THE LEAP OF REASON

by

DON CUPITT

THE WESTMINSTER PRESS
PHILADELPHIA

Published by The Westminster Press ®
Philadelphia, Pennsylvania

PRINTED IN GREAT BRITAIN

Library of Congress Cataloging in Publication Data

Cupitt, Don.
  The leap of reason.

  Includes bibliograpical references.
  1. Knowledge, Theory of (Religion). 2. Pluralism.
3. Ethical relativism. 4. Revelation. I. Title.
BL51.C84   120   75-44180
ISBN 0-664-20749-9

For Susan

Contents

Contents

Introduction

Attempts to understand religious belief are usually made from some one point of view; that is, on the basis of some philosophical presuppositions. For the plain man, these are the general assumptions of his *milieu*, held in common and unconsciously. For the philosopher, they may be Kantian, empiricist or whatever, consciously held and defended. But in this book I am not asking what religious belief looks like from one particular point of view. Instead I am studying the problem created by the extraordinary *diversity* of points of view from which people see the world; the problem of pluralism, which is, in the end, a religious problem, with wide ramifications, political, epistemological and moral.

All of us, in one way or another, confront it: we have to strike some kind of balance between loyalty to the group's way of looking at things, and the affirmation of our own freedom. Each of us belongs to one (and probably nowadays to more than one) group, which has its own belief-system and value-system, its own entire way of looking at the world; but at the same time we have to transcend the group's way of looking at things, in order to affirm our own individuality, and also so as to deal fairly with others whose perspective on life is quite different. For example, I am an officer in two distinct institutions, the Church and the University. The former requires of me allegiance to a particular structure of symbolism, form of life and way of thinking; the latter exalts the spirit of free critical inquiry. So my situation obliges me to distinguish between a sense in which the self is culture-bound, tied by a particular and concrete pattern of allegiance; and a sense in which it must nevertheless transcend that particular claim. But, *formally*, my situation has many parallels nowadays, for we are all conscious, within ourselves and in our social relations, of the variety of perspectives upon the world.

Traditional philosophy sought to establish the objectivity of knowledge by appealing to reason or to fact; but now we hear it argued that standards of rationality are themselves culturally relative, and that there is no 'pure' factual discourse, or even sense-experience, prior to the culturally relative conceptual frameworks through which we apprehend the world. These startling claims are no longer advanced as philosophical speculations, but as established positions in many branches of the sciences of man. The linguistic claim is that the forms of language determine the forms of thought, so that the whole world-picture of a society is shaped by the form of its language. The sociological claim is that the patterns of social relations determine the way the universe of experience is constructed. Put the two together, and the suggestion is that linguistic, social and cosmographical structures are interdependent parts of a single whole. It is paradoxical that, in the century of 'one world', many should be coming to think that there is *not* one world, but only a diversity of socially constructed worlds. But how can we even *say* this, unless we can transcend our particular social and linguistic *milieux*?

There is a middle way to be sought here. If I allow the collective belief-system under which I live to become absolute, I fall under its tyranny; but if I absolutize the spiritual freedom which enables me to transcend it, I become a kind of nihilist, and society begins to disintegrate. How can we steer a course between dogmatism and scepticism, tyranny and anarchy, loyalty to culture and spiritual freedom?

You will see how the argument runs in what follows. Working away at the problem of relativism, we unfold a philosophy of spirit. To the distinction between the culture-bound empirical self and the free spirit there corresponds a distinction between the affirmative and the negative ways in theology. I argue that a theistic philosophy of spirit, belief in God, strikes the right balance between society and freedom, between the duty to affirm a cultural perspective and the duty to transcend it.

Never has it been so important to strike that balance. Looking ahead, we see crushing burdens of overpopulation, economic and social stress, and national and ideological rivalry. There will be attempts to impose tight social discipline for the sake of survival, and there will be desperate revolt against it. Tyranny or anarchy, that seems to be the choice. And what is the prospect for the individual freedom which you and I have enjoyed? The kind of freedom capitalists believed in is doubtless doomed. What kind of freedom should men of religion and philosophers strive to preserve? What kind of freedom is the *sine qua non* of human life? That I try to say.

To the main argument I have added three essays, in order to show the theological implications of it. They were all first written as lectures, and later published in *Theology* (S.P.C.K.). They are reprinted here, with amended titles and some corrections, by kind permission of the Editor.

PART ONE

The Leap of Reason

1

Reason and Pluralism

Everyone likely to see this book lives in a pluralist society: a society, that is, in which it is publicly acknowledged that there are entrenched and apparently unsettlable differences of approach to and belief about fundamental questions of morality, religion, politics, and some other topics. And nearly all of us like to have it so. We are so glad to have the freedom to form and defend our own opinions on these matters, that we are very willing to pay the price of daily hearing other people express utterly different views.

But there is an obvious difficulty. How can we each hold fast to our own particular set of moral and religious beliefs while at the same time professing to accept and even welcome the fact that in our society such issues are regarded as inherently disputable and unsettleable? Must not a pluralist society drift towards relativism or subjectivism? For suppose I hold some moral opinion on a matter of great importance, how can I at once hold it for true with a full and rational assent and yet, in the same breath, courteously allow that of course everyone is entitled to his own opinion, and I shall have no reason to reproach you if it turns out that yours is quite different from mine? Am I not almost contradicting myself?

In the nineteen-sixties progressive theologians were labouring to prove that religious believers can live comfortably in a basically secular society. Perhaps they can, but our present question is a harder one than that. To believe in reason is surely to believe that important disputes can be settled by rational argument. Whether our ancestors were Jews, Christians, or Muslims, they believed in one absolute intellect, and so in one final truth, to which the human intellect might at last attain. But this old alliance of reason and monotheistic faith is at odds with the assumption of modern society that there *is* no single final truth in questions of morality, religion, art, politics, and the like. Indeed, if to accept pluralism is to accept that there cannot be any final truth in such questions, then pluralism is essentially atheistic.

Of course, this same society in which we live is founded materially in a high degree of rationalism in mathematics, and in pure and applied science. But that only makes the contrast with the state of affairs which prevails in matters of belief and ideology all the more glaring, especially as mathematics and the sciences appear to owe their present splendour precisely to having prudently steered clear of all such matters.

It is an uncomfortable situation, which most people resolve in a rough-and-ready way by allowing mathematics and the sciences a near-monopoly of rationality in the public sphere, the sphere of the objectively demonstrable; and by regarding matters of religion, morality, and the like as matters of free private judgement. The individual may in these realms opt for what is true 'for him', but it is only true-for-him, subjectively true. If he is able to articulate and express his personal orientation with sufficient artistic ability[1] he may, by this appeal to the imagination, persuade others to adopt his outlook; but an objective, universal and rational justification of his opinions is not to be looked for. If it were to be produced, plural- ism would be threatened : but we like pluralism, so we would prefer it not to be produced. Yet the effect is surely to 'psychologize' religion and morality, to make them merely subjective, and rob them of all intellectual seriousness.

As pluralism develops it presents awkward problems to those who make and enforce the law. The law has been supposed worthy of general moral respect because it expresses the moral consensus of society. But what if there is no general consensus? If society is sharply divided, what are law-makers to do? And what becomes of the jury system? The old assumption was that any twelve good men and true picked at random could be relied upon to form a competent jury. Shall we concede nowadays that the defendant has a right to demand trial by a jury composed of people of his own sex, race, class, moral or political outlook, religion, or whatever, and that he is justified in claiming that he will not receive a fair trial unless this demand is met? Clearly pluralism may become a threat to the social consensus and public spirit which make the rule of law possible.

And yet, broadly speaking, we like pluralism, and would hate to be thrust back into a form of society in which there is but one comprehensive belief-system endorsed by the state-power, and pur- veyed ceaselessly by all the organs of public information. We like

[1] It is typical of today that preachers of new doctrines have given place to novelists who make fashionable new 'lifestyles'.

pluralism for good reasons, because it is in many ways a great and remarkable moral advance. One might even say that it is one of the most remarkable achievements of modern culture.

It developed in two stages. The first is *diachronic pluralism,* or the historical consciousness: the realization that past ages really were very different from the world of today, and the consequent attempt to enter sympathetically into the minds and the world-views of men of past epochs. Sir Walter Scott is usually, and perhaps rightly, credited with being the pioneer here. The second stage is *synchronic pluralism*: the realization that contemporary men living in other cultures have different world-views from ours, which can be entered by an effort of sympathetic imagination. Their religion need not be regarded as 'idolatry', or 'superstition', or as a demonic parody of ours. Their technology need not be regarded as childish, nor their ways of thinking as 'prelogical' or 'primitive'. Their culture as a whole does not need to be measured and judged by standards derived from our culture, but can be explained as from within and in its own terms. The history of comparative religion, ethnography and anthropology shows how laboriously, and through what fierce controversies, these insights were gained. And since in Western countries we now have, willy-nilly, men of a great variety of races and religions coexisting, the anthropologists' insights are surely a great and socially very necessary moral advance. It is not as yet a very secure advance, for the average man is much less tolerant and pluralistic in outlook than the intellectuals who stand, more or less, in the liberal academic tradition. But the latter group presumably hopes and expects to convert the former, given time.

Yet what of the *relativism* implied here? Certainly it is a remarkable achievement, without precedent in earlier centuries, that works of art from nearly every human culture, present or past, can find admirers and be marketed to them in London, Paris, and New York; that the traditional drama and dance of Japan, India, Georgia, and the Niger Basin can be performed in the same cities; and that the worship of nearly every major religion can be discovered going on in London every week. But what of the relativism which is surely implied by this new catholicity of taste and outlook? Walter Scott would not have tried to re-create the past, and his public would not have wanted to enter it in imagination, unless they had felt a certain dissatisfaction with the present. The nineteenth century would not have been so industrious in establishing and filling museums unless men had felt that the most splendid arte-facts of the past were unlikely to be surpassed in the future. It is only in modern times, since Beckford and Soane perhaps, that rich men have collected old things on a large scale; previously they would have commissioned their own contemporaries. Would we conserve old buildings as determinedly as we do if we still thought, as men once did, that we could pull them down and build better? Would a canvas by Rembrandt be worth a million pounds, if men thought that better ones were being painted today?

Perhaps our pluralism is only so generous as it is because we have lost confidence in ourselves. Of course, diachronic pluralism developed earlier than synchronic, because for much of the nine-teenth century the Europeans thought that although they were, after the Industrial Revolution, admittedly smaller men than the giants of Renaissance Italy, they were still much more 'improved' than the stagnant cultures of the East and the 'savages' of Africa. But in due course even that confidence wavered.

Is pluralism, then, linked with irrationalism and a disastrous loss of morale? We should not, of course, make the common mis-take of supposing that widespread scepticism is a sign of impending doom. The Greeks were sceptical, and so were the men of the Renaissance. So was Shakespeare. But the Greeks were a little like us. Their ancestry was mixed and their religion eclectic. Through their zest for travel and trade they mingled with men of a wide variety of cultures, and this led them in the direction of relativism and moral scepticism. Eventually they had innumerable philoso-phical sects, mystery religions, and mountebanks of every des-cription—like us. It could not last: sooner or later the idea of one rational God and one truth, divine and human, must impose itself to restore order.

But the obvious difference between them and us is the enormously greater strength of our science and technology. And to under-stand the peculiarly debilitating character of modern pluralism, so far as matters of belief are concerned, we must consider for a moment the issue of the value-neutrality of science. For the com-mon opinion is right: it was in the seventeenth century, and it was with the rise of modern science, that a permanent split first appeared in European culture.

The age we live in has, on the whole, rejected the idea of divine knowledge as the supremely important kind of knowledge by which men should guide their lives, and has instead put its trust in the scientific attitude and a publicly established body of scientific knowledge. And the puzzle is this: how can the scientific attitude and body of knowledge be an effective guide to life, if from the first it was based on a conscious exclusion of 'final causes' and moral ideas? Whether in the seventeenth century or today, the dilemma is urgent: the world-view of natural science has in the main professed itself to be value-neutral. How then can science *guide* us? Is not scientific knowledge, by itself, as useless and potentially pernicious as Plato held rhetoric to be? Rhetorical skill was a kind of technical virtuosity, which gave one the power to move one's fellow-men, but an education in rhetoric alone was useless unless one also learned to what end its power should be directed. Correspondingly, scientific knowledge has put great power into our hands; but this power has been gained by the deliberate exclusion of all questions of values and ends of action. To get the power which scientific knowledge gives you, you must pay the price of being deprived of the knowledge of how it should be used. Science will give you the strength of a giant; but a blinded giant.

One or two familiar examples may be given. We hear quasi-scientific talk nowadays about 'pollution'. Unfortunately pollution is not a scientific concept, but an evaluative, and indeed originally a ritual one. One can easily expose the confusions with a few simple questions, such as, 'Is the Dead Sea polluted?', or 'Are elephants causing environmental damage by uprooting trees on the East African plains?' To talk about 'pollution' or environmental 'damage' is to appeal to a contrast between the way things are in fact going, and the way in which they ought to be going, and that 'ought' cannot be derived from purely indicative scientific statements. And if the drift of modern biological science is towards insisting that man is part of nature, then there cannot be any *scientific* reason why the effect of man on the environment should be described as 'pollution' and the effects of elephants, sheep and volcanoes should not be so described. I am not saying that 'pollution' and 'damage' are not important ideas: of course they are important. But I am saying that they cannot be purely scientific ideas, if science is indeed so value-neutral as it has been supposed to be.

Another example: it seems possible that the physical basis of homosexuality is now being discovered. It has to do with the levels of certain hormones during pregnancy. Homosexuality, it is announced with some pride, will soon be 'curable'. Whereupon militant homosexuals indignantly reply that their condition is not a disease, but is perfectly 'normal'. The dispute seems not to be scientifically solvable, and we come to realize that medicine is saturated with evaluative terms, such as *healthy, sick, pathological, disease, normal, natural*.[2] But of course medical men (until very recently) received no training in ethics, and like other practitioners in the sciences of man, they have been trained in a scientific method which is unconsciously mystifying. That is to say, the entire teaching and practice of the subject has systematically, if not deliberately, concealed the fact that these terms are evaluative, and so has confused thought.

The same thing happens with even more grotesque results in psychology and sociology when people fancy that ethical problems can be dissolved if only ethical words are replaced by supposedly descriptive terms like *mature, well-adjusted* and *anti-social*.[3]

But enough of these examples: our problem is, how can the rational man guide his life by science alone (as Freud, for example, vehemently insisted he should) if science is professedly value-neutral? We can see the dilemma emerging in the seventeenth century, but there is an even earlier example in Nicolò Machiavelli's *The Prince*, written about 1515: 'The chief foundations of all states ... are good laws and good arms. And as there cannot be good laws where there are not good arms, and where there are good arms there must be good laws, I will not now discuss the laws, but will speak of the arms.'[4]

Machiavelli's words recall Plato's characters Callicles (in the *Gorgias*) and Thrasymachus (in the *Republic*); or they may recall Stalin's scornful inquiry about the Pope's military capability. But he is not being facetious, nor is he being deliberately immoral. He is rather amoral, in that he sees it as a duty rigorously to exclude ethics from

[2] Homosexuality is, by the way, an interesting example of the general problem of this book: for with it, as with schizophrenia, there are strong arguments for regarding it as having 'natural', biochemical causes; and also strong arguments for regarding it as a socially caused condition. The boundary between nature and society is breaking down.

[3] For a typical attempt to eliminate ethics, see Barbara Wootton, *Social Science and Social Pathology* (London, 1959). See pp. 338f., where she suggests that medical men are seizing the moralists' old territory today, much as in the nineteenth-century geologists and biologists captured territory previously ruled by the Book of Genesis. A writer who is aware of some of the dangers here is Thomas Szasz, in *The Myth of Mental Illness* (New York, 1961), and subsequent books.

[4] 12; trans. Luigi Ricci.

statecraft. Hence the admiration felt for him by many modern political scientists: Machiavelli's modernity consists in his belief that by leaving morality out of the question one is being more 'objective' and 'realistic'. The state is a system of forces to be manipulated by the Prince and his advisers in the interest of personal and national (the two coincide) power and security. Statecraft becomes a *technē* as objective as ballistics, but with the result that Plato would have foreseen; for the method by which Machiavelli has developed a technique for the manipulation of political power has deprived him of any way of stating to what ends it should be directed. Power is to be increased, but to what end? The gaining of more power? To what end? The gaining of more power yet.

This is precisely the thought-situation in which apologists for technology used to say, and may perhaps still say, 'Progress is inevitable.' A technology without rationally chosen goals has nothing to do but accelerate into hypertrophy and destruction. The increase of purely descriptive and technical knowledge, purchased at the price of leaving out values, can issue only in an ethic of fatalistically accepting the 'trend'. It is but a short way now to the bizarre twentieth-century ethic whose only moral duty is the duty not to moralize; and the confused society which gives the highest moral authority to the people with the least moral awareness or training.

Even Spinoza says something of the kind in an unfinished treatise found in his desk when he died in 1677:

And that I might investigate the subject-matter of this science with the same freedom of spirit as we generally use in mathematics, I have laboured carefully, not to mock, lament, or execrate, but to understand human actions; and to this end I have looked upon passions such as love, hatred, anger, envy, ambition, pity, and the other perturbations of the mind, not in the light of vices of human nature, but as properties, just as pertinent to it, as are heat, cold, storm, thunder, and the like to the nature of the atmosphere, which phenomena, though inconvenient, are yet necessary, and have fixed causes, by means of which we endeavour to understand their nature ...[5]

You may grumble about the weather, but your time would be better spent in the study of meteorology, for the fluctuations of the

---

[5] *Tractatus Politicus,* 1, §4; trans. R. H. M. Elwes.

weather have fixed and ascertainable causes; and you may praise
or blame human behaviour, but your time would be better spent in
the study of psychology, for the vagaries of human behaviour have
likewise fixed and ascertainable causes. So Spinoza's analogy suggests, and indeed part of my citation from him was used by G. W.
Allport as the epigraph to one of the best modern textbooks of
psychology, *Pattern and Growth in Personality* (New York, 1961).

It is not surprising that the wars of religion in the sixteenth
century should have created scepticism about the certainties in
whose name they had been fought: you could hardly have more
sceptical men than Montaigne and Shakespeare. Their age and
that following were times when men were sceptical, inquiring, fascinated with power, on the make, and confident of their own
abilities. They wanted to know about efficient causes, and they
wanted an end to mystification. And this climate of opinion at least
helped to frame the scientific attitude. The change was not seen
at first as a matter of religious certainties crumbling and being
replaced by scientific certainties: 'New Philosophy calls all in
doubt', said John Donne in 1611, because the new natural philosophy itself was also still a battleground of conflicting theories.
While Copernicus and Ptolemy contested as equals it seemed
reasonable to require that they be studied side by side at Oxford,
as Sir Henry Savile demanded. So you might even argue, as Milton
presumably did, that while this uncertainty prevailed the old
scheme of things remained essentially intact. Plato was right: certainty lay in theology, not physics. It was fun to while away an hour,
as Adam and Raphael did in *Paradise Lost*,[6] arguing the merits
of rival cosmographies: but in the face of eternity such disputes
were comparatively trivial. The knowledge of God still remained
the chief end of human life, and moral obedience was more important
to man than speculation about celestial motions.

But as the New Philosophy gained in confidence, religion and
morality were set aside as Sunday concerns by men whose weekdays
were dedicated to achieving a complete analysis of the universe
in terms of matter, motion, and number. At first men claimed
that the new philosophy was no threat to the old religion, and held
that it was theologically orthodox that they should separate faith
and reason in the way they did. But motives were mixed; for
the separation might be pious, but it was also convenient and pru-
dent, and in time it became plain that the language in which it was

[6] Book VIII, 66–178.

being justified ran very close to the language of mockery. It is often hard to tell whether a man is being serious or sarcastic; as, for example, in the following series of statements:

... the more absurd and incredible any divine mystery is, the greater honour we do to God in believing in it; and so much the more noble the victory of faith.

Methinks there be not impossibilities enough in religion for an active faith.... I desire to exercise my faith in the difficultest point; for, to credit ordinary and visible objects, is not faith, but persuasion.

... it is with the mysteries of our Religion as with wholsome pills for the sick, which swallowed whole, have the vertue to cure; but chewed, are for the most part cast up again without effect.

... the Christian Religion not only was at first attended with miracles, but even at this day cannot be believed by any reasonable person without one.

If we consider the words of these statements alone it is surely impossible to tell which speaker considered himself a believer and is speaking seriously, and which is speaking in mockery. Their authors are, respectively, Bacon (*de Augmentis,* IX), Browne (*Religio Medici,* IX), Hobbes (*Leviathan,* 32), and Hume (first *Enquiry,* X). And there is real doubt, concerning more than one of these men, whether *he* knew whether he was a believer or a scoffer.

But this oddly veiled transition, from piety to mockery, is all-important. Modern science began, in the seventeenth century, in an attempt to make a fresh start, to be 'philosophical'; and to be philosophical meant to set aside questions of revealed religion and morality. Only in an age already sceptical about religion and morality could men have dreamed that so to set them aside increased one's chance of a true understanding of the matter in question. But they did so dream. At first lip-service continued to be paid to the old faith, sometimes doubtless sincerely, but in terms which are verbally scarcely distinguishable from the open sarcasm into which, by the eighteenth century, it had degenerated. Since the divorce of science from morality and religion had paid such obvious dividends, few were able or willing to question it. In

some cases the decline into religious scepticism was masked by a
stratagem borrowed from Plato: one claimed to have discovered
a philosophical religion spiritually superior to popular religion,
which one was then free to ridicule. Some of these philosophical
religions, like Spinozism, Deism, or Hegelianism, were splendid
structures; but they did nothing to arrest the drift towards scepticism.
They rather hastened it.

The process we are describing has been very long drawn-out.
The world-view of the natural sciences has only attained complete
dominance in our culture in the present century, so that only now
are we seeing fully displayed the social consequences of ideas
which were first put forward several centuries ago. And the most
important of these ideas is the claim that the method and temper
of the natural sciences is the only sure way to knowledge.

It is of course possible to understand this claim in a tautologous
sense; for *scientia* in Latin, like the French *science* and the German
Wissenschaft, just means organized knowledge, methodically built
up. The modern, narrower sense of *science* in English only appears
in the earlier nineteenth century. The tautologous sense of the claim
that science is the only way to knowledge gives place at about
that time to the bolder claim that the scientific method, at last
becoming clearly conscious of its own distinctiveness, is the only
way of building up that edifice of knowledge by which a rational
man guides his life.

Now in the general anxiety to avoid a collision it has commonly
been said that there can be no conflict between science and religion
because science is systematically neutral as regards questions of
morality and religion. I hope our discussion has made it clear that
this is facile and misleading. In the first place, the very claim that
in the pursuit of truth questions of religion and ethics can and
should be set aside is itself linked, historically and in logic, with
a measure of scepticism about them. People call Machiavelli
'scientific' or 'realistic' precisely because of his attitude to morality.
Secondly, if the sciences are really as value-neutral as they pretend,
how on earth are they able to perform the influential guiding
function in our society that they evidently do perform? And finally,
the enormous success and power of the natural sciences has gained
for them monopoly rights over the word 'science' itself, and a
near monopoly of publicly acknowledged rationality and objectivity,
in a way which reflects very unfavourably upon the standing of
ethics, theology, politics, and other 'non-scientific' subjects. As one

might expect, efforts have been made to put the study of these subjects upon a 'scientific' footing; and the very modest results of such efforts have not helped matters either.

So, far from being neutral, the sciences, and especially the sciences of man, have in a curious way accelerated the movement towards pluralism and subjectivism in matters of belief and ideology. Yet, as we have also argued, these same sciences are not and cannot be as value-neutral as they have historically professed to be. If we look to them for *guidance*, then we cannot suppose them to be purely descriptive.

There is a final twist in the argument. Since T. S. Kuhn's *The Structure of Scientific Revolutions* was published in 1962 there has been a certain invasion of science itself by relativistic and sceptical currents of thought.[7] The situation whereby the sciences appeared majestically rational and objective, while the arts languished in confusion, was too good to last for ever. I will briefly pick three strands only out of the argument.

First, as the history of science has developed it has become obvious that it cannot be treated in isolation from the history of religion, politics, economics, technology, and so on. Scientists of the past were men of their time, and their scientific judgements betray the influence of 'ideological' factors proper to their period. An obvious example is the setting of Darwinism in its historical context in nineteenth-century economics and politics. But if the science of the past was thus influenced by 'ideological' factors of which men were at the time largely unaware, the same may presumably be true today.

Secondly, Marxism is the single most influential ideology in the world today, and it is strongly relativistic. All thought is seen as relative to the prevailing economic conditions and material circumstances of life. Marxism has been particularly critical of liberal ideas of objectivity. Everyone has an 'ideology', whether he knows it or not.

And in the third place there is much in the sciences of man which may well be thought to generate scepticism about human rationality. Many anthropologists seem to talk as if the individual's life and thought were entirely determined by the society in which he lives. Many sociologists speak as if a reasonably complete causal explanation of people's beliefs and behaviour can be given in terms

[7] Anticipated, of course, by such philosophers as the later Wittgenstein, and R. G. Collingwood.

of their social circumstances and the like. Many psychologists appear to hold that a reasonably complete causal explanation of the individual's beliefs and behaviour can be given in terms of psychic factors. But these patterns of explanation can scarcely be stopped from extending to the person who proposes them, and then to the science which he and his colleagues are developing. We said earlier that when it is applied to man the scientific method focuses attention on the causes, rather than the grounds, of people's beliefs and behaviour; and so hastens the tendency in our culture to subjectivism in religion, morality, and so on. But if the tendency is to treat our religious and moral beliefs as 'rationalizations' or 'projections', perhaps our scientific beliefs may suffer a similar fate. What is sauce for the goose is sauce for the gander. If medieval theology is rightly judged to have been an elaborate ideological validation of the power and wealth of the medieval Church, then by the same token one might equally argue that modern physics, its successor as Queen of the Sciences, is an elaborate ideological validation of the power and prestige of modern physicists.

In this chapter I have sketched our present cultural situation, and said why I believe pluralism is a real threat to belief in reason. The central problem is that of the supposed value-neutrality of the sciences. Though in many ways the empirical sciences deserve our deep respect as the principal remaining stronghold of belief in reason, it has to be noted, first, that their development has accelerated the slide towards relativism and subjectivism in matters of religion, morality, art, and politics; and, secondly, that the way the scientific method is being applied to man may lead to an undermining of science by science. This is a new form of the paradoxical scepticism about reason described long ago by Hume: 'reason ... furnishes invincible arguments against itself'. In what follows I shall try to establish a philosophy of spirit which yet retains the valuable features of modern pluralism.

2

Is Religious Truth Subjective?

We have suggested that in a pluralist society religious truth readily comes to be seen as being merely subjective. This suggestion needs to be explained, and I have to show how plausible it is. For at first glance it is at variance with the language and the claims of the religions themselves. There never was a religion which did not most emphatically claim to be the true religion. Its doctrines are the true doctrines, its rites are divinely ordained, and only within its fellowship and by its law can true salvation be won. Every religion makes such claims—on its own behalf.

Faced with the diversity of religious doctrines, and the vehement claims made for them, it is to be expected that anthropologists should offer explanations in 'naturalistic' terms of how it comes about that religions are believed true. They offer, first, a *causal* explanation, running something like this: man, helpless in a terrifying world, personifies the unknown powers that be in the hope of learning to control them. The way he does this reflects the child's experience of learning to cope with adults. The form of a society's religion is intimately linked with the methods by which children are socialized in that society, and since there is such a link between the socialization process and the religion the two come to confirm each other. The patterns of social life both give religious belief and practice its shape, and provide experiences which seem to confirm its truth: and religion in turn reinforces the patterns of social life.

Secondly, anthropologists may offer a *functional* explanation of why a religion is practised. Belief in gods, and the performance of rituals, meet needs: cognitive needs, like the need for meaning; practical needs, like the need for rain or for victory in war; and motivational needs, like the need for the relief of anxiety, guilt, or dread. In so far as a religion, and only it, can succeed in meeting these needs, it will be deemed true by the worshippers.

Such are the ways in which an anthropologist may explain the rise and persistence of religious institutions, institutions which he may see as 'consisting of culturally patterned interaction with culturally postulated supernatural beings'. Religion is a cultural product, socially caused and socially verified.[1]

The philosopher would prefer to approach the question of the truth of religious beliefs in a different way. He does not at first see the truth of religious beliefs in terms of their social origins or their social utility. He asks whether a religious belief is justifiable in the sense that the believer understands it (as being about a god), rather than in the sense in which an anthropologist-commentator understands it (as a projection or symbolic expression of certain social relations). For surely we ought to begin by taking people's statements at their face value, and only under very strong pressure conclude that they are 'really' statements about something else altogether.

But the trouble is that if we are talking about the truth of *religion* it is not too easy to keep the philosophical and anthropological ways of thinking distinct. This difficulty will recur as we proceed.

First, however, let us pursue the philosophical approach. Now, the meaning of truth is in a way a simple matter. As Aristotle says in his *Metaphysics*, 'to say of what is not that it is, or of what is that it is not, is false; while to say of what is that it is, or of what is not that it is not, is true.' Aldrich is more succinct: 'Vera est quae quod res est dicitur'; and Tarski is equally brief: 'The statement that p is true in a certain language L if and only if p.'

In a way this is indeed simple. p is true if and only if p. But now, what about the *application* of this scheme, what about the criterion of truth?

One suggestion is that of the plain man, that we may check whether p is true by comparing it with the fact which it states, or the state of affairs which it designates. There is a correspondence, an isomorphism, between a true fact-stating proposition and its objective matter. Truth consists in the presence of this isomorphism.

[1] See the article by Melford E. Spiro in Michael Banton (ed.), *Anthropological Approaches to the Study of Religion* (London, 1966); and E. R. Leach, *Political Systems of Highland Burma* (London, 1954), p. 14: 'Ritual action and belief are alike to be understood as forms of symbolic statement about the social order.' (Cited in Rodney Needham, *Belief, Language and Experience* (Oxford, 1972), p. 6.) But it should be added that many anthropologists now are wary of formerly popular causal and functional explanations of religion. See, for example, E. E. Evans-Pritchard, *Theories of Primitive Religion* (Oxford, 1965) for a vigorous attack upon them by a senior anthropologist.

But this does not take us much further, even supposing the task of defining the conventions of representation to have been accomplished. For we have only succeeded in specifying the conditions under which the proposition has meaning in the sense of mirroring or picturing that state of affairs which it designates. It still remains to be said how we can check that what a proposition asserts to be so, is so.

For what kind of exercise is it to lay out a proposition alongside a fact to see if they are of the same shape? Whoever does this? Would it not be safer to leave out those dubious entities, facts? Nobody knows what they are, and there are all the puzzles about negative facts, conditional facts, and so on. Perhaps we can answer the question of the criterion of truth by referring instead to the logical relations between propositions. To ask about the truth of *p* is to ask about the logical relations between it and other propositions—relations such as entailment, compatibility, corroboration, contrariety, and contradiction. In this way we can avoid the puzzles caused by the claim that truth is a special sort of property possessed by all true propositions. To say that *p* is true is to do no more than assert *p*. And to justify your assertion of that *p* you must do more than simply draw attention to its possession of a certain odd property. What you must do is to produce evidence and arguments for *p*.

However, I am convinced that a purely logical account of truth will not do: at some point there must be an extra-logical check. However otherwise could we decide between two coherent systems of propositions, incompatible with each other? This is notoriously the situation we find ourselves in when comparing two religious belief-systems.

So there is much to be said for the empiricist solution, which is to link meaning and verification very closely. To understand the meaning of a position is to know how to put it to use and to test it; and to determine its truth is simply to carry out the test. If I assert that the time is now 5 p.m., you could not even understand me if you had no idea at all of how to discover the time. You may possibly not know how time is represented on clock-faces, but you must have *some* idea of how to verify my assertion.

Any account of truth, then, must make some reference to states of affairs, awkward things though they are. And the questions of meaning and truth are bound up together. I know what a proposition means when I know what state of affairs it designates, and how to ascertain whether or not that state of affairs actually obtains.

Unfortunately not all questions of meaning and truth are as clear cut as those raised by my assertion that the time is now 5 p.m. For it seems evident that there are propositions whose meanings are not fully specific, and in respect of which conclusive truth-testing is not possible. But they are worthless unless we can say *something* about their meaning, and they are at least *candidates* for truth, in that they can to some extent be confirmed or disconfirmed by the appropriate kind of evidence. Theological propositions seem to belong here.

Philosophical considerations, then, suggest that the problem of the verification of religious beliefs is going to be difficult. But if we add in the anthropological considerations it is made more difficult still. For anthropological functionalists will still insist that religious beliefs are projections, under certain stresses, of certain social facts. The beliefs are socially generated, their real meaning is social, and they are confirmed in a circular way by the same social facts which gave rise to them. This circularity is a warning against any simple appeal to religious experience in verification of religious doctrines, particularly as the theologians who make this appeal are often the same ones who say that religious experience generated the doctrines!

MORAL TRUTH

It is sometimes suggested that religious truth is moral rather than logical. For if we describe as *true* a religion or a god or a rite, we are using the term in a way more like its use in the phrase 'a true friend' than its use in the phrase 'a true assertion'. And it is certainly the case that, like the term *meaning*, the term *truth* and its cognates are extensively used outside a strictly linguistic or logical context. In the case of truth the term *fact* illustrates how the gap between statement and thing is leaped. If you make some questionable assertion and I ask, 'Is that true? Is that a fact?', you would be hard put to it to say whether my query is about your assertion or about the thing referred to in your assertion. The words *truth* and *fact* slip about between being used of assertions and being used to refer directly to the actual states of affairs asserted to obtain.

Let us then call the truth of persons and things, of gods and rituals, moral truth. Now in many languages we have a strong suggestion that moral truth is an older and more fundamental concept than what might be called logical truth. Students of biblical theology are alleged to be fond of detecting national character in lexicographical details. If so they will certainly be impressed by the words for truth. For the English words *true* and *truth* are related to the words *trow*, *troth*, and *truce*, suggesting loyalty to a covenant, the fidelity of a gentleman whose word is his bond. The Latin *verus* suggests reliability and solidity, not to say stolidity. And the Greek *aletheia*, unconcealment, suggests that the crafty Hellene may once in a while throw off his habitual dissimulation and speak openly.

Here then we have a family of ideas—of constancy, candour, fidelity, trustworthiness, and genuineness. Truth has moved from the utterance, not this time to the state of affairs the utterance picks out, but rather to the speaker. Its antonym is not *falsehood* so much as *falsity*. If a man is true we may take it that he will be candid and open in his utterance.

There are many idioms associating the true with the real or genuine. What is true is contrasted with what is spurious, counterfeit, fictitious, or unrepresentative of the type. The man who is true is straight or upright and not crooked or twisted or bent; he is authentic and not an impostor. A structure is true if the walls are perfectly vertical and the courses of brick or stone horizontal. A bell cast without a flaw rings true. The naturalist talks of a true specimen of a species, or of the true indigenous species in contrast with what is deviant, variant, cultivated, or imported. Conformity to an ideal kind is suggested by the phrase 'true to type'. Truth in the sense of reality is contrasted with figments, misleading impressions, and appearances. A representation or appearance is true to life if, under certain conventions of representation, it adequately represents what it portrays.

Two further groups of idioms are important for religion. In so far as reality is thought of as organized in grades there may arise talk of the Truth, the whole, absolute or final Truth as contrasted with relative or partial truths. And there is an important metaphorical use of ringing true: in literary criticism we may say that a passage of writing *rings true*, an idiom not easy to explain but undoubtedly relevant to any description of the way people make up their minds about religion.

Now many of these 'moral' senses of truth are echoed in religious language. And so we hear it argued that the Bible is not concerned with the Greek notion of logical truth, but always and entirely with moral truth. Moral truth is the older and more fundamental concept. Then it is said that moral truth is related to logical as subjective to objective. And so it may be argued (in the existentialist manner) that religion is not at all concerned with theoretical or speculative truth, but only with what is morally, existentially, and subjectively true *for me*.

There is an obvious fallacy in this argument. If I call Peter a true friend my assertion has no descriptive force unless you can infer from it propositions to the effect that he tends to behave in some ways and not others on certain occasions. And my assertion that Peter is a true friend is not itself true unless some of these predictions are fulfilled. Propositions in which moral truth is predicated do not gain any special exemptions thereby: they may themselves be true or false. So there is a confusion in saying that faith is entirely interested in assertions such as 'God is true' and not at all interested in whether assertions about God are (logically) true or false.

But the mention of the phrase 'true for me' does remind us that there is nevertheless a *prima facie* case for regarding religious truth as subjective in another sense, which we must consider. For it is plain that both the man who propounds a religious doctrine and the man who assents to it have an interest to declare. They both stand to gain. This interest is so strong that it must cast doubt on how much concern for truth really counts in religion.

TRUTH AND POWER

When the officers of a religious institution promulgate a religious doctrine on behalf of that institution, what are they doing? If we think about religious beliefs in the concrete situations in which they are urged and adopted we cannot fail to notice the connection between truth-claim, claim to authority, and power. The man who has made a convert has gained in power; and the convert has gained membership in a group. An alliance has been made.

There is an example of the connection in the late S. G. F. Brandon's book, *The Creation Legends of the Ancient Near East*,[2] amplifying the thesis of an earlier essay in the S. H. Hooke *Festschrift*. Brandon argued that a cosmogonic myth has the function,

---

[2] London, 1963. The classical examples of Brandon's thesis are the rival sacred cosmologies of the oldest Egyptian cities.

among other things, of advancing the interests of the sanctuary which propagates it. The site, and perhaps the foundation, of the sanctuary may be mentioned in the myth. The myth is about the beginning of the world, but it is also a claim that in a certain sanctuary a true experience of the divine is to be had. Behind the telling of the story lies the claim to spiritual authority of a particular sanctuary and its priesthood. The 'truth' of the myth is bound up with the sanctity of the shrine, the efficacy of the rites performed there, and the authority of the priesthood established there since the world began.

It has for a long time been the stock-in-trade of anti-clericals that religious bodies invariably regard as orthodox that teaching which furthers the interests of their officers, and as heterodox that teaching which is hostile to those interests. There is an amusing example in the fifth of Voltaire's *Philosophical Letters*. Since the honour of God and his priest are bound up together, the determination of what is to count as orthodox is invariably reserved by the clergy to themselves.

In modern times ecumenical negotiations have been found by painful experience to have in many cases the character of a struggle for power between two rival priesthoods, each jealous of its own status. The negotiating teams on both sides are largely made up of clergymen, and discussion centres upon the doctrines of the Church, ministry and sacraments, doctrines in which the interests of the clergy are particularly at stake. Indeed those doctrines have been framed to promote those interests. The ideal solution is the one requiring the fewest concessions by the parties, and the fullest recognition possible of each by the other. The rules of the game demand that the parties profess a deep concern for truth, for issues of principles and matters of conscience; but this is a masquerade. For the real aim of each party is to defend the authority and validity of its own priesthood and to make no admission which would let its own side down by betraying any lack of confidence in its own 'heritage'.

At a less ignoble level the interest of the religious group colours not merely its ideology of itself, its officers and its rites, but its entire theology. And this is a more subtle question.

In Christianity, the fundamental doctrines of the Trinity and the Incarnation were formulated in the controversies of the fourth and fifth centuries. The principles or axioms guiding the development of thought were derived from the basic claim that the salvation enjoyed within the community by believers was genuine and final. The true religion is the religion which gives believers a true experience of God, and binds its adherents indissolubly to him. Orthodoxy is that account of Christ and God which best articulates the claim that in the Church and there alone true salvation is to be had. The sacraments really unite the believer to Christ, and Christ is nothing less than God himself incarnate, so that there could not be a more adequate saviour. The whole man is wholly redeemed, so that Christ must be wholly human. The life which animates the community can be nothing less than the life of God himself, so that the Holy Spirit is divine too.

One cannot say that there was *no* other interest to be borne in mind. The discussion was conducted within certain limits; there were metaphysical beliefs, and there were premisses derived from the community's traditions. But within those limits the main interest was in obtaining a satisfactory conceptual expression of the community's conviction that within itself, and there alone, was true salvation to be had.

Many theologians make a virtue of this. They see the theologian as the servant of the Church. He articulates and defends its faith, and serves its interests. He presupposes that the interest of the Church and the interest of truth coincide. But I am bound to say that history makes one sceptical about this, even though in practice a saving corrective is often introduced, by distinguishing the Church's true interest from what some members of it at some time may consider to be its interest.

If we next turn to the believer, he is surely bound to say, 'I believe the doctrines of this Church because I have found salvation in it. This Church is the true Church, its priesthood the true priesthood, its rites the true rites, and its doctrines the true doctrines.'

But now we can scarcely avoid the question of subjective and objective truth, for the believer seems to be saying, 'It is true, because I have found it to be true *for me*.' He seems to have come to a point beyond argument where he says, 'Now I know, I was seeking and now I have found, I am content, this for me is *it*; it is true for me in such a way that I must regard it as the truth, true without qualification.'

Are we to be halted by the maxim that religious truth is subjectivity? How can it be decided whether the salvation offered within a particular religious community is the genuine article? There are of course criteria for distinguishing illusion from reality in religious experience; but the criteria are developed and are applicable only *within* the community. The criteria themselves presuppose faith. What are we to do about this?

SUBJECTIVE TRUTH

Most of us, when confronted by vigorous religious faith which we do not share, try to treat it with respect and would be willing to say that it is true for the believer. His beliefs express his way of responding to the world and give a framework for moral action, and may do this very well; but we feel we can acknowledge this without supposing that the beliefs of Mormons or Scientologists have the same sort of claim upon our assent as our ordinary empirical beliefs.

But what do we mean by saying that a sincerely held religious belief is 'true for' the believer?

In 1960, at the height of the Macmillan era, John Bowen published *Storyboard*, a light novel about advertising, the morality of which was much discussed at the time. There is an interesting conversation in it in which a girl who works for a big agency endeavours to defend her profession. She describes a campaign on behalf of a rheumatism remedy called Amipax. Now in copywriting you may not lie. Anything you state as a fact must be a fact. Rheumatism is incurable, and in any case patent medicine advertising is not allowed to promise cure. Rheumatism is at least partly psychosomatic. People want attention, and rubbing helps. Amipax was a mild local anaesthetic, and it gave people a pretext for being rubbed.

The copywriters had to make Amipax sound as if it might be a cure, so they promised 'quick relief', which was true. People bought Amipax, and wrote letters professing to have been cured by it, which the agency's own Legal Department would not let it use. But if the agency had said candidly, 'Rheumatism is incurable, but rubbing in Amipax will make you feel a bit better for half an hour', the media would have refused the copy and the public would not have bought the product. So 'quick relief' was the formula used.

After explaining all this, the girl concludes by saying, 'So what's the truth? Seems to me there are as many truths about that kind of thing as there are people.'

The copywriter took the public's illusions at their own valuation and was able to help—on that level. To have set out to dispel the illusions would have been a hostile act, and of no help. The ambiguity of the copywriter's language must match the ambiguity of the needs he seeks to satisfy.

Enter a large chemist's shop and contemplate the range of branded products stacked on its shelves. Almost none of them gives any measurable physical therapeutic benefit, but our need of illusions is itself a real biological need. We need reassurance and consolation, a need which we need to portray to ourselves as a physical ailment which can be physically remedied. We need to feel that we are slim, tanned, fair-haired, regular, fragrant, clear-skinned, and lovable, and the products aim to help us feel so. So far as they do, they are in a sense genuine.

Are the anxieties and longings which religion assuages—the sense of sin, the characterization of all the objects about us as contingent, the longing for perfect love, the quest for meaning— similarly ambiguous? Amipax confers a real benefit which people can sincerely attest, by an illusory meeting of an illusory need (using the word 'illusion' in the Freudian sense). We need only grasp the difference between the overt and the real character of both the need and the remedy.

Here is a level at which religion could be recognized as genuinely beneficial, just as a doctor might in good conscience refrain from disillusioning someone who truly felt better for the use of Amipax. And the question of objective truth need not be raised.

The copywriter says, 'If you and your conscience rob people of their illusions you will not benefit them, you will merely rob them of the real comfort they can be given by taking their illusion at its own valuation. The illusion has real biological value, it reduces suffering. People have needs, they want to be happy, the copywriter wants to make them happy, and so he uses pictures of babies to sell soap. The act of buying and using this soap becomes an expression of mother-love, and why not? Mother-love is good, it is good that it should be expressed, and the soap whose use is an expression of mother-love is better for people to use than soap chemically identical which lacks these associations.'

It is not for nothing that the Church has both advertised its concern for truth and been willing to accommodate itself to mankind's need for illusions. It has been willing to temper the wind of new knowledge to the shorn lambs of the flock, and to look indulgently upon pious practices which are theologically dubious.

Institutional religion professes to be concerned for truth, and yet sees very strong reasons for compromise in practice.

I remember a young clergyman, green and serious, who conscientiously refused to have anything to do with the children's nativity play in his parish, on the ground that the Church should not officially encourage such a grossly sentimental and fictitious portrayal of the birth of Jesus. He scandalized the congregation for being so needlessly rigorous, especially where children were involved, and found himself in deep water. We teach children delightful fictions, especially in connection with Christmas. Why deprive them of this innocent pleasure? He saw it as an issue of truth, they saw it as a moral issue; so he and they between them divorced the claim of truth from the claims of charity. He was being, it was said, immature and gratuitously unkind to the children. Perhaps we agree that he was being needlessly troublesome, but if we do then we agree with the copywriters and the churchmen in putting moral and pastoral considerations above the claims of truth—or, more fundamentally, in separating these two interests.

And what of the question of fact? Does not religious language, even in the hands of a sophisticated and indeed honest preacher, have a built-in tendency to seem to promise more than it will actually deliver? It seems to promise deliverance from dread and guilt, peace of mind, joy, communion with God, moral victory, the perpetual protection of a loving heavenly father, and even victory over death. Those who hear and believe the promises will later testify that they have gained something, but they will be hard put to it to say what. For they still suffer anxiety, dread, turbulence of spirit, and moral perplexity. They affirm they are under the protection of an all-powerful Father, but I do not think they would claim that this is reflected in a measurable way in their health, accident, income, or actuarial statistics. Some naive religious people do make such claims, but they embarrass the rest just as the Amipax agency was embarrassed by its testimonial letters.

And even if there is some empirical evidence—as there is—of a favourable correlation between religious conviction and practice and psychological stability, it seems to be a correlation with the act of believing rather than with the objective content believed. The Mormons are an outstanding example of a religious body which delivers the goods in terms of social cohesion and psychological stability, but few would wish to credit this to the intellectual merits of the Mormon doctrines. It is your faith in the product which cures you, not the product itself; the believing, not the content believed.

Finally, the faith that Amipax is therapeutic is at least partly self-verifying. William James points to cases where 'faith in a fact can help create the fact', and Russell says that 'mysticism creates the truth it believes in'; and from such a starting point the question of objective truth becomes irrelevant.

TRUE RELIGION

There is, then, a *prima facie* case for regarding religious truth as subjective in the sense described: and it is so regarded, on the whole, in a pluralist society like ours.

It is a fact which no theologian should wish to deny that there has always been a good deal of illusion in the actual practice of religion. Illusion arises because we demand subjective truth, and give it priority over objective truth: and it is encouraged all the more when we are led, by our society, to suppose that objective truth is not to be had.

Nevertheless, the religious quest is an attempt to free oneself from illusions, and make true for oneself only what is true in itself. We shall try to show how this can be done.

3

Absolute Knowledge

I have been describing the way pluralism threatens the traditional belief in reason and the unity of truth as if it were quite a new problem, and indeed the distinctive problem of modern culture. But it would be truer to say that it is a new form of an old problem. Plato and the Buddha were exercised about very similar issues. That this world is in a state of endless flux; that it offers no lasting satisfaction to the intellect or the affections; that no absolute knowledge of it is possible, only relative and transient belief—these were platitudes in Greece and India twenty-five centuries ago. Both religion and philosophy—and they were not very different activities—were concerned with showing men how they could transcend the flux of this-worldly existence and lay hold on eternal blessedness. A typical set of doctrines about how this could be done is the following:

P1 Besides our ordinary sense-based beliefs about the natural world around us there is another and higher kind of knowledge.

P2 The gaining of this higher kind of knowledge is the chief end of human life.

P3 Its possession brings four benefits: it provides answers to the great riddles which surround human life; it provides remedies for the great evils of life; since, once it is gained, it is gained eternally, it brings with it eternal happiness; and its possession sets one on the path to moral perfection.

P4 It is to be gained by following a certain moral and intellectual discipline.

P5 It is intuitive, and not discursive, and consists in the intellectual contemplation of one or more transcendent and eternal objects.

P6 This contemplation is possible because we have within us an immortal and divine part of us, the Rational Soul, whose proper home is the intelligible world. By it we can rise above the phenomenal world of change and decay.

P7   Through this contemplation the Soul gains mastery over the passions, and so the four benefits mentioned in P3; for it is bondage to the passions which dooms much of human life to suffering and futility.

I have labelled these seven doctrines P1–7, because they are commonly thought of as 'Platonic'. How far we can directly assert that they are simply Plato's own views is a matter for expert judgement, but they seem to me to be so.[1] At any rate they have been interwoven with the history of religion and philosophy in the West, and something very like them occurs in the East as well. So prominent have they been that Marxist atheism has chosen to direct against them the main thrust of its attack on religion. It sees in this set of doctrines the typical expression of man's perennial but mistaken attempt to escape from the flux of this-worldly existence.

Yet in fact it is doubtful how far P1–7 adequately represent the intellectual nucleus of religion. Here, for example, adapted from William A. Christian (*Oppositions of Religious Doctrines*, London, 1972), are sketches of the principal themes of Buddhism and Judaism respectively:

B1   Nirvana is the supreme goal of life.

B2   Aim at attaining Nirvana.

B3   The Dharma is the path to the attainment of Nirvana.

B4   Live in accord with the Dharma, in the community of the Sangha.

B5   The good life is a life in accord with the Dharma.

B6   Attainment of Nirvana is the only way to gain release from suffering, which is caused by desire, which is in turn intrinsic to conditioned existence.

B7   The Buddha is the supreme exemplar of the above doctrines. He himself attained Nirvana under the Bo-tree; and his teachings, and the body of tradition about him, are the authoritative expression of the Dharma.

And now Judaism:

J1   God is holy.

J2   Respond rightly to God.

J3   The Torah teaches us how to respond rightly to God.

J4   Live in accord with the Torah, in the community of Israel.

J5   The good life is a life in accord with the Torah.

J6   God is the creator of all things, and all men belong to him and are accountable to him.

---

[1] At least, in the *Republic*.

J7 Moses, who led Israel out of bondage in Egypt, received the Torah from God on Mount Sinai.

As is evident, B1–7 and J1–7 are here arranged in a corresponding order, so as to bring out the formal resemblances and differences between the two faiths. How far these sketches are accurate and uncontroversial is disputable: perhaps it is impossible to characterize a religion in a way which will satisfy everybody, and I have myself altered Professor Christian. The only point I require to make is that someone who accepted and lived by B1–7 or J1–7 would surely have a claim to be called a religious believer, Buddhist or Jew as the case may be; but in neither case is it clear that acceptance of the religious doctrines entails acceptance of P1–7 in full. Indeed, although Buddhism and Judaism are very different faiths they seem to have more in common with each other, structurally, than either has with Platonism. Both the B-doctrines and the J-doctrines contain a mixture of elements. There are evaluative statements (to the effect that something is of supreme worth); there are statements of belief; there are practical recommendations (directing one where to live, in what community, and by what principles); and there are historical statements by which the doctrinal system is tied to a community and its traditions, including traditions about the key events and personalities through whom the community came into being. This mixture of elements is, I think, typical of a system of religious beliefs, and it is rather different from the mixture we find in P1–7. In the religious systems metaphysics is less conspicuous, and greater prominence is given instead to practices and techniques, and to the community with its historical traditions, its sacred Law, and its exemplary lives and stories.

It seems, therefore, that P1–7 is not a particularly good translation into philosophical language of what the religions are after. So far as mankind has hungered after absolute knowledge, it has expressed (and perhaps satisfied) this need very largely through one or other of the religions. P1–7 represent a very bold philosophical elaboration of the claim that there is absolute knowledge, and it is of supreme worth: but it is not the only way in which such a claim might be or has been articulated. The Hebrew Bible, for example, undoubtedly witnesses to a religion, but the P-doctrines are scarcely present in it at all.

The incompatibility between the Platonic doctrines and religious doctrines is equally striking in the case of Christianity. Its historic insistence that God cannot be directly and intuitively known in this life directly contradicts Platonism. It emphasizes the community [cf. B4 and J4]; it emphasizes certain historical events, an Exemplar and Saviour, and a body of teaching derived from him and his immediate followers [cf. B7 and J7]; and like Judaism it affirms the created world and the passions [cf. J6]. The frequent combination of Christian with Platonic doctrines was always a *tour de force*, and always sooner or later a cause of strain.

What is more, Platonism is to some extent to blame for our present cultural discontents. In antiquity Platonism fell at last into scepticism. Separating the world of eternal values from the world of transient fact in the way it did, it robbed the former of empirical anchorage, and the latter of stability and moral worth. Correspondingly, the Platonism of the early Renaissance degenerated again into scepticism by the seventeenth century, eventually to leave the world of nature at the mercy of an expressly amoral and mechanistic natural philosophy.[2] So Platonism's separation of the world of value from the world of phenomena to some extent anticipated the scientific attitude. And the Platonic divorce between reason and the passions, between the active and contemplative lives, and between the worlds of fact and of value, is still to this day reflected in strains within our own culture.

It has often been said, and with some justice, that religion is the common man's metaphysics, and metaphysics is the religion of the intellectually gifted. People who devise, and people who are attracted to, metaphysical systems have very often wanted to dissociate themselves from the religion of the vulgar. Metaphysics has been an esoteric religion purveyed to a small circle of intellectual aristocrats, and its doctrines have been shaped by that function. The man who accepts P1–7 is assured by those doctrines that he is superior to the average man who works with his hands; that he belongs to an élite group of leaders who know things beyond

---

[2] Marxists rightly drew attention to the contrast between bourgeois culture and the heartless mechanized world in which the industrial proletariat had to live, and connected it historically with Platonic metaphysics. But they were too much in love with natural science to see how seventeenth-century natural philosophy had helped prepare the way for the worst evils of industrial society. Indeed Marxism ratifies, rather than questions, the metaphysical presuppositions of industrialism. Merely abolishing bourgeois culture and giving him high social status is an altogether insufficient answer to the complaint of the factory worker, as the experience of socialist countries is showing.

the ken of the masses; and that he has achieved a special degree of self-mastery.

There are, then, religious, cultural and political reasons for suspecting the Platonic doctrines; yet so influential have they been that it seems to many that if they are given up, then the whole idea of absolute knowledge of a transcendent object must be given up with them. David Hume was one of the first modern thinkers who expressly renounced the traditional idea of 'divinity' as absolute knowledge which bestows blessedness. In more recent times there have been many attempts to interpret religion in non-metaphysical terms. But the resulting accounts of religion have been felt to leave out the heart of the matter by plain men as well as by philosophers. So I propose now to give a first sketch of an alternative account of divine knowledge which is neither Platonic nor reductive. The sketch will be in the form of a parable which will show how the problem of transcending the limits of this-worldly existence can remain of central importance, even where it is not claimed that direct knowledge of the transcendent is to be had.

Imagine a man confined in a prison which has no doors or windows, and which he has never left.[3] He knows only the prison. His world is his immediate surroundings, and for him it is *the* world. He is, perhaps, a member of a small community of people living their lives in a quiet and orderly way within this closed environment. Their language does not contain words like 'confinement', 'prison', 'wall', and 'boundary'—or if it does, these words are related to states of affairs within the prison, and are not used to characterize their situation as a whole. Indeed, philosophers among the community might insist that though it makes sense to speak of enclosed spaces *within* the realm of their experience, to speak of the world as a whole as an enclosed space has no meaning. There is a language barrier against any attempt to understand and speak of their situation as a whole. And so most of the community live most of the time in a state of enchantment. The sages among them pretend to be the spokesmen of common sense and the *status quo*, while in fact being the magicians who make it their business to maintain the general enchantment and rebuke anyone who threatens to wake up. Over and over again

[3] My story is a temerarious attempt to correct Plato's allegory of the Cave.

they insist that the concepts 'here' and 'outside' only have meaning within the world, and cannot be used to transcend the experienced realm; with such effect, that dreams of escape come to seem like a kind of madness. So the common people become habituated to living in a prison and not recognizing that it *is* a prison. Indeed, they quite forget to think about such things, for there seems little reason to do so. Their world is effectively a closed and self-maintaining physical system, in which everything is recycled. They have forgotten even to speculate about the ultimate energy source from which their world is supplied. While it was still necessary the sages insisted that such speculation was empty and profitless, until at last there was so little perplexity that they scarcely troubled to discourage it any more.

Yet one day the man we are thinking of suddenly does awaken. One day he speculates that the world may be bounded. He imagines that his world as a whole may be a 'here', 'inside', in contrast with a wider realm 'outside', 'yonder'. He feels an uneasy thrill, for he knows how strongly common sense and public opinion would rebuke him if it was known what he was thinking, but the very forbiddance of his thought is an incitement to pursue it.

How can he develop his barely grasped thought of 'outside', when the established use of language so strongly obstructs his thinking? He may say that 'outside' is ineffable or incomprehensible, by way of noting that language and thought are by now so adapted to the world here that they systematically oppose any attempt to speak or think of yonder. So he will have to begin by saying that 'outside' is not like here. Next he may say that 'outside' encompasses and is greater than here. In the third place, he may suggest that 'outside' contains the reason for or the explanation of his confinement here. Were he to escape, then from his vantage-point 'outside' he would be able to look back and see more clearly the nature of his previous confinement. Finally, he may imagine that there may be others like himself 'outside', but nobler, freer, and wiser, as would be fitting in their ampler world. To them he and his fellows would appear to be in a state of enchantment or sleep.

These four lines of thought were called, in the old terminology, the ways of negation, eminence, causality and analogy. The act of mind by which our prisoner thinks 'outside' might be represented as a passage from sleep to waking, bondage to freedom, darkness to light, death to life. At least, he himself might wish to use his imagery. But if he betrayed his thoughts to his companions, they would think him at best an idle dreamer, at worst plain mad. For them it is *he* who is captivated by an illusion, not they.

The act by which he thinks 'outside' is a strange and complicated one in which conceptualization, postulation, and aspiration are all simultaneous and inseparable. As soon as he thinks of his world as bounded, as soon as he *de*fines it, he experiences it as *con*fining and aspires beyond it. Discontentment and hope, postulation and aspiration, arrive at once. For him, outside is both ideal and actual. The successive ideas, *this world, bounded, here, outside,* are yoked to their correlative states of speculation, discontent, aspiration. The whole complex intellectual process arrives with such a rush that it seems like a flash of intuition, or revelation.

But he is sure to have doubts. He is perplexed by the curious frailty and emptiness of the concept of 'outside'. It seems to exist for him only as the shadowy correlate of 'here'. To say that it is unlike 'here', that it is greater than 'here', that it contains the reason for his confinement 'here', and that out there life must be suitably larger and nobler, is to say next to nothing. What he can say with confidence about 'outside' seems so slight that he wonders if he has a solid idea at all.

Rather more substantial is the difference which the bare ability to conceive 'outside' has made to him and his situation here inside. He is a changed man, not so much because he has information about 'outside', but rather because his attitude to his world inside has become completely different. He was sunk in a world which was complete for him, and which gave him no cause for dissatisfaction. Now he feels like an alien. In a sense he is worse off, but he would not revert to his previous innocence even if he could. He has become more highly conscious; he is aware of himself as spirit.

Still the doubts persist, and they fasten next upon his other discovery, the idea of 'here'. There may or may not have been some fact about his environment which triggered off the idea. If the prison has a boundary wall, a perimeter, we can imagine him comparing it with partition walls that divide spaces within the prison, and reasoning by analogy that there is correspondingly a space beyond the boundary wall. But it may be that his world does not contain such obvious 'signals of transcendence'. It might be like the surface of a sphere, finite but unbounded, so that in traversing his world he never stumbles against anything that so readily suggests the idea of 'outside'. Facts about the world which suggest a beyond are, in any case, controversial: a fact which seems suggestive of transcendence to one person may not seem so to another, and arguments either way are often inconclusive.

So whether or not there is a feature of the world which acts as a trigger and occasions the idea of its contingency or finitude, doubts will still arise about the status of 'here'.

It seems, in the first place, that 'here' is not defined ostensively —or at least, not in any ordinary sense. Usually, if we are explaining the meaning of a concept by pointing to things, we not only point out such-and-such things to illustrate what we mean, but also exclude other things. This and this are examples of yellow things, and that and that are not. In the case of 'here', however, our prisoner points to everything and excludes nothing. Indian sages, teaching the meaning of 'Brahman', say, 'It is within all this, and it is beyond all this', with a sweeping gesture. I suppose the same sentence and gesture are also teaching the meaning of 'all this', for 'all this' is also a metaphysical rather than an empirical concept. Our prisoner does not first grasp 'here' empirically, and then infer 'outside'. He needs the dawning here–outside contrast to be able to grasp 'here'.

Nor does 'here' seem to be a scientific concept; at least, not necessarily so. It depends upon the guiding assumptions on which science is usually done. Certainly it is possible that the prison-scientists, taught by the philosophers, should work upon the assumption that their world is a closed and complete physical system. We can imagine them making observations, performing experiments, and connecting up causal chains into cycles, so that their results tend to confirm the presuppositions which have been guiding their work. If scientific work is guided by the assumption of an autonomous physical system, nothing contradicting that assumption can become entrenched. When some such thing does appear, it is regarded as an *anomaly,* which must be eliminated by being brought under a *nomos,* a law. If it cannot so be explained, it is simply left out of the system of scientific knowledge. Thus the scientific idea of the world as a closed physical system is an unconscious and regulative idea, of a different kind from our man's 'here'. It is used to *exclude* the wonderful, not to create a sense of wonder. It is used in a highly conservative way, to ratify the common assumptions of society, not to question them.

Another suggestion might be that 'here' is inferred by our prisoner from the disparity between his desires and what his world will allow him to achieve. He may feel that his powers and his wishes are greater than the world about him can satisfy, and imagine that in a larger world outside they might find an adequate scope. However, sceptics retort that the insatiability of desire is mere biological fact and that it is a misinterpretation to draw metaphysical inferences from it. The longing for eternity is merely the biological need to struggle as hard as possible to preserve one's life as long as one can; the longing for 'outside' is merely the biological drive to capture and command as large a territory as one can. In a competitive world we would not have survived so long and come as far as we have, had these drives been less peremptory.

A fourth suggestion about the concept of 'here' is that it is arrived at not by observation or inference, but by a voluntary change in the prisoner's attitude to himself and his own situation. 'By relating itself to its own self, and by willing to be itself, the self is grounded transparently in the Power which posited it.'[4] His new insight has been made possible by a practical change in the way in which he looks at himself-in-his-world. However, from the psychological point of view, it seems that the dawning here–outside contrast comes first and then creates the practical change, rather than the other way round. And in our analogy, in which we are considering our prisoner's situation from an authorial standpoint outside, *we* at least can see clearly that a question of fact is involved. It might be replied that our prisoner's friends inside cannot, logically cannot, see that a question of fact is involved, because all their thinking and language are conditioned by their being inside. Could they understand what we, you the reader and I, are thinking about them? Is that not precisely the point at issue? The prisoner's becoming able to see that a question of fact is involved is precisely his achievement, precisely what marks him off as a metaphysician among positivists. In thought at least, he has leapt out of his situation and joined us, you and me. He has made the leap of reason.

One can understand this amphibious existence in the aquarium at the zoo. We the visitors stand in a darkened room looking through a glass wall into an illuminated aqueous world. Great dreamy turtles and shoals of fish drift about, oblivious of us. They are in their world and we in ours, and they have no reason to suspect our existence. For them, our world is not. Then a keeper in a frogman suit, bearing a bucket of small fish, walks past us through a door and shortly appears in the tank. Its denizens crowd round him, snapping at the food. He has entered their world and is part of it, but we know

[4] S. Kierkegaard, *The Sickness unto Death* (1849), 1, i (trans. Lowrie).

that he also belongs to ours. Here is, for a moment, a signal of transcendence; we are prompted to think 'the world' because within it we encounter lesser worlds, each relatively self-contained; and there may on occasion be passage between one lesser world and another, as when a man enters the underwater world.

A similar leap is made, as our citation from Kierkegaard reminds us, in self-consciousness. It is a fact that in self-consciousness a man can 'climb above' himself and look down upon himself, making himself the object of his own thought. For example, I may 'see through' my immature opinions of some years ago. Or I may both take full responsibility for some past action and at the same time repent of it. I do not disown the action or choose to forget it: no, it was my action, I expressed myself in it, and I identify myself as the one who performed it. Repentance is not throwing off, leaving behind, or discarding one's past self. It is rather an affirmation that one really is that self. What I was, I am; but I condemn what I was and am. I do not throw away what I was, I keep it, it is still me; but I add to it tears, build upon it, and so transcend it.

Thus the past is another world within the world which may suggest to our prisoner the idea of transcendence. Others include the world of the dead, the world of dreams, and the worlds of imagination.

But however fully the prisoner tries to elaborate and explain what he means by 'here–outside', he is going to have difficulty in explaining himself to the sceptical sages.

The difficulty is that the mental act by which he thinks 'here–outside' is unique, so it is hard to see how he can ever formalize it in a valid argument. The point is this: any argument to prove the existence of 'outside' needs to have two properties. Its premisses must be true, and its form must be valid. If its form is valid, the terms in its premisses must be replaceable by symbols which stand for variables. These variables may, in turn, be given other values, yielding other valid arguments to true conclusions. That is to say, if there is to be a sound argument for the existence of 'outside', one would expect there to be other formally identical sound arguments proving other similar things. But this there cannot be, because the prisoner's 'outside' is *ex hypothesi* a unique idea. There is nothing else remotely like it: there cannot be. So all the prisoner can do is to go on talking to anyone who will listen. He can only describe; he cannot prove.

So the prisoner keeps coming up against a peculiarly intractable difficulty in his own position. Perhaps he would do best simply to affirm that intractability; to insist on the scandalous oddity of his dream of awakening. Certainly he must resist the patronizing suggestion that his difference from the others is a 'subjective' difference, for to say that a difference is subjective is to shrug one's shoulders and toss it into a rag-bag of superstitions, prejudices, rationalizations, and other inexplicable beliefs.

I have told a parable to show something, but not all, of what religious belief is about, and to illustrate its peculiar ambiguities. Who, in the parable, is in bondage to false ideas, and who is freed by the truth? Who is the dreamer, and who awake? The parable situation differs from 'Platonism' in that there is most definitely no chink in the prison wall, and we do not postulate that our prisoner has any extraordinary faculties. So he has no direct knowledge of 'outside': only his own heightened consciousness, the leap of reason. The parable is—or should be—evocative, because it is so close to many of the sources of religious imagery—waking from an enchanted sleep, being lost in a magic wood, being redeemed from bondage. Indeed, philosophers and saints have often sought small enclosed spaces, by way of creating the parable-situation so as to see the issues more clearly. It is perhaps for this reason that so many great ideas and books have emerged from exile, from prison, from persecution, from monastic cells and small closets.

So much for our parable, whose purpose is to suggest pictorially the philosophy of spirit which is to be established. In what follows, when I speak of *spirituality*, I mean the capacity in men for a 'leap of reason' of the kind which figures in the parable.

We have to prove the *applicability* of the parable, in order to prove that a man can be spirit. This will be attempted in what follows. But if you are prepared to allow that the parable is *intelligible*, then that is something. The prisoner's colleagues would not admit even that much.

4

Seeking and Finding

There are various ways of describing the supreme goal of metaphysics. The Platonic tradition, as I have called it, seeks absolute knowledge of an absolute object. I have rejected this ideal, without troubling to rehearse the classical criticisms made by the British empiricists and Kant, because, as I have argued, it is in any case not what the religions are saying; though in fact I do substantially accept the Kantian critique. Another way of describing the goal of metaphysics is that of Hegel: it seeks the absolute autonomy and self-sufficiency of the self-conscious spirit. Without rejecting this idea (yet), we have chosen a very modest starting point, namely our bare ability to become conscious of the problem of the limits of thought.

I am claiming that this starting point, though it will lead to a philosophy of spirit less grandiose than Plato's or Hegel's, is more in accord with what the religions have historically claimed; and, as will appear in due course, is more directly relevant to our cultural situation.

When, in the last chapter, we were describing Buddhism and Judaism (and alluding to Christianity), we noticed a structural similarity among the basic doctrines of these great religions. The doctrines relate the object of aspiration, the law, and the community of believers to each other, somewhat as follows:

R1 P is of supreme worth.

R2 Direct your life towards P.

R3 L (the sacred Law, a system of practical directives, exemplary stories, etc.) is the way to P.

R4 Live in accordance with L.

R5 The good life is a life in accordance with L.

R6 A life in accordance with L is ultimately, because of the way things are, the only finally blessed and profitable life for a man to live.

R7 Live this life in a community, C, dedicated to it, which is the trustee of a tradition of L derived, at some time in the past, from an authoritative source.

Since the faiths in question are very different from each other, and yet have this structural similarity, I claim that we have here the typical nucleus of a religious belief-system. The three main things in it are P, the supreme object; L, the sacred law, writings and traditions; and C, the historic community.

It is a common feature of religion that P is in one way or another said to be transcendent. It is beyond the reach of language. It cannot be known directly or described in a straightforward and matter-of-fact way. What it is must be suggested indirectly by negations and by analogies. Yet it is more than any analogical representation of it. The best way to learn what it is is to live by L and in membership of C; for the concrete religious system, the whole comprised by all the elements of L and C, prescribes to the believer imagery, ways of thinking and living and of imaginative response to life through which as a whole he will apprehend something of what P is.

L and C together, introjected within the proficient believer's consciousness, and made the pattern of a habitual way of thinking and approach to life, make up what I shall hereafter call an *interpretative framework*, or more simply, a *programme*. Any comprehensive world-view, as it is adopted and made somebody's philosophy of life, is such a programme, whether a religious one or not.

The feature of religion which I want to notice at the moment is this: a particular religion proposes a particular programme to the aspirant believer. It says that he must enter and make his own a particular complex of images, rules, concepts, and so on. It proposes its particular programme as the authoritative way to P. But it is careful to insist that even P-as-disclosed-by-this-authoritative-programme is still not P itself absolutely. A great religious tradition asserts its own relativity. *Thus the ancient religious recognition of the relativity even of religious knowledge constitutes an early recognition of the problem of the relativity of all our knowledge.* Indeed it is to religion that, historically, we own the consciousness of the limits of thought, a consciousness which in religion is the mark of a truly spiritual believer.

More of all this in the sequel. Now since to enter a religion is to adopt a total programme for life and thought, it is clear that the principal condition for attaining religious knowledge is a conversion of mind and life.

The intellectual conversion required to enter upon religion has something in common with the wit needed to see the point of a joke. One does not perceive P immediately, and directly judge it to be of unsurpassable worth, by applying to it the canons of judgement which have served one hitherto. Rather, it is aspired after by people who have come to see the absurdity of all else. So a sense of futility, absurdity, or enslavement is felt at an early stage in the religious quest. Mocking himself and his petty concerns, a man begins to wonder what would make him take himself and his life seriously. As Kierkegaard rightly saw, a sense of the comic is at bottom a sense of the absurd incongruity between the finite and the infinite. Like the prisoner in our parable, the man who would understand religion has to be prepared to make a peculiar mental jump to a new standpoint—rather like the one needed to see that the joke is on oneself. A common image is that of soaring in imagination and looking down from above upon the scurrying absurdity of oneself and one's world.[1] From this new standpoint his whole life looks different: his use of language changes correspondingly, and the resulting rupture in his thinking readily gives rise to talk of inspiration, revelation, or miracle.

Moral conversion follows a parallel course: from the new perspective his life hitherto seems worthless, because the canons by which he judged things were wrong. At an earlier stage he felt only a sense of remorse or futility. This may have been a useful preparatory disposition, but it is not in itself of any religious value. Now something more substantial appears, repentance, in Greek, *metanoia*, a change of mind, a deliberate correction of his system of values. This may be willed once and for all, but it is only fully realized in a life by the study of L and the gradual bringing of one's thought and conduct into habitual accordance with L.

This laborious undertaking is encouraged by steeping oneself in the typical pattern of response, the philosophy of life and the historical traditions which the religious community fosters and guards. These are also part of L, and they count among the things a person should have studied if he is to be considered proficient in the faith.

[1] Since this imaginative soaring can occur in mild narcosis (for example, with nitrous oxide), or in dreams, it is not surprising that many religions have made use of narcotics and dreams. Something like it occurs in mania, too, so that madness has been thought to be divine or demonic possession. Compare also the interesting religious experiences reported by several of the men who have seen the earth from the moon.

But it does not follow, from what I have said, that 'only insiders can understand', as is sometimes claimed by religious apologists who wish to protect their beliefs from any possibility of refutation. Religious subjectivism may take the form of a claim that a religion is a complex way of thinking and living which can be understood only by participating in it. Some people who use this gambit invoke the authority of the later Wittgenstein. The criteria for meaning and truth in a religion are internal to that religion, and there is no external, objective standpoint from which it can be appraised.

This doctrine appears to be mistaken. I can understand Marx's writings without being or becoming a Marxist, Freud's without being a Freudian, and Spinoza's without being a Spinozist. Any great thinker who has created a complete world-view of his own demands an effort of sympathetic imagination if one is to understand him, and of course he is not easy to criticize. It would need considerable talent to write a good imaginary conversation between Spinoza and Marx. It is plainly true that in the writings of someone like Spinoza the terms he uses derive their meaning from the part they play in his system of ideas as a whole, so that it is not easy to argue with him. But it has been done, and people have surely understood him without having been converted by him. We can, and do, get a good deal of pleasure from trying on strange ideas in imagination, rather as one might dress up in strange clothes and look at oneself in a mirror. An account of the logic of religion which denies this power of the imagination is highly misleading. For, as we have stressed, such an imaginative act is necessary if one is to be able to take up a religious perspective on life at all.

Nor does it follow from what I have said that in religion one is required to believe things without evidence, or to give to doctrinal statements a greater degree of assent than is warranted by the evidence which can be adduced in support of them. The statements R1–7 above are of different kinds, and to defend them all would call for several different kinds of argument. In any great religious tradition one can find highly elaborated patterns of argument by which the basic doctrinal evaluations, recommendations, and assertions are explained and supported. Doctrines which are in principle incapable of justification ought not to be believed.

It will still be retorted, however, that the methods by which doctrines are justified and the criteria of meaning and truth are, or are asserted to be, internal to the system of beliefs. We shall discuss the question of the 'truth' of an entire programme shortly, in a larger context, because one may well reply that if this objection is valid in respect of the justification of religious doctrines, it is also relevant to psychoanalysis, to Marxism, to ethics and, for that matter, perhaps, to natural science as well.

My immediate purpose is to rebut the arguments that 'only insiders can understand' and that 'religion calls for belief without adequate evidence'. These two arguments have perhaps arisen because of a mistaken appreciation of the relation between the moral and the cognitive sides of religion. People have taken it that the religions are saying that they and only they who obey and live by L and in C will come to the truth, and that *this* in turn means that you must first take something on trust in the hope that subsequently the grounds for it may be vouchsafed to you. Moral commitment must come first, and understanding follows later.

It is not quite like that. We must begin analysis of the relation between a programme and what we are able to perceive through it. These are two quite different things, often confused in the use of such an expression as 'world-view'. But they must be sharply distinguished, if we are to make any progress with the question of the 'truth' of a religious or other belief-system.

The first example I shall take in order to analyse the issue is that of *the meaning of life*, a phrase which has attracted some philosophical notice lately. Our object is to discover and show the proportion between imposed meaning (the meaning one puts *into* life by moral endeavour and by patterning one's life ethically) and perceived meaning (the meaning which is disclosed to one *by* life).

THE MEANING OF LIFE

Because modern English-language philosophy has been much exercised by problems of meaning, the rather portentous phrase 'the meaning of life' has caused a certain amount of irritation. Some philosophers would like to cut it down promptly by asserting that the word 'meaning' itself only has meaning in linguistic contexts.

Can this be done? The best attempt to produce a purely linguistic definition is as follows: to specify the meaning of a linguistic expression is to produce another linguistic expression which, on some occasions at least, can be substituted for it without changing the force of what is said. Two linguistic expressions mean the same when they can be used to perform the same speech-act. This attempt fails, because it says only what it is for two expressions to have the same meaning, not what it is for an expression to have a meaning. And in any case, the definition was obliged to refer to the accomplishment of a purpose or the performance of an act; that is, it made reference to a non-linguistic entity, namely a speaker, intending to accomplish something by his speech.

Linguistic meaning, then, cannot be defined without reference to a speaker's purpose in speaking. Newman once remarked that 'We speak our meaning with little trouble; our voice, manner and half-words completing it for us; but in writing, when details must be drawn out, and misapprehensions anticipated, we seem never to be rid of the responsibility of our task.'[2]

Newman's use of 'meaning' here shows clearly how the meaning of language depends upon the purposes of speakers. People mean to do things: that much must be admitted. But need we go any further? Can all that we may reasonably say about the meaning of life be expressed in terms of the meaning we put into our lives, the purposes we set ourselves to achieve?

It seems that talk of the meaning of life can be grouped under three headings:

1 *Meaning as purpose and worth*

The first and clearest meaning of meaning is undoubtedly purpose, aim or intention. Someone's life is worthwhile and meaningful if he has a body of long and short-term projects which cohere in a morally satisfying whole. He may or may not be thought to need a single overriding purpose to take up and unify all the subultimate purposes.

But the passive voice is also used, when someone asks what he is cut out for, or meant for. Here he thinks of a larger drama or scheme of things in which he has to discover and play his part. The language used may be impersonal, and perhaps pessimistic or ironical (destiny, fate); or it may be personal (vocation, calling). In this latter case the ideal is a coincidence of active and passive purposings, for the caller calls, not only through external circumstances, but immanently through the make-up of the one called. The one called feels at home in the world, properly adjusted to life, when what he means to do is identical with what he is meant to do. There is a just proportion and match between imposed meaning and perceived meaning.

Some existentialists have nevertheless urged that the onus for

[2] *University Sermons* XV, 17.

giving meaning to my life rests entirely on myself. If my life's work collapses, or I die prematurely, my life is in that case irretrievably meaningless. Against this, the theist insists that a man cannot, without risk of a ludicrous collapse, set out to make his own life worth while. Meaning must be received and appropriated, not just posited. It is true that only I can make my acts morally good, but it does not follow that only I can make my life valuable. For the value of a man's life is more than the sum of the values of his acts. For example, quite apart from questions of religion, if someone has died prematurely in tragic circumstances, his friends may resolve to complete his incomplete life by ensuring in various ways that fresh and valuable consequences shall continue to flow from his having lived. In this way they set out to make sure that he has not lived in vain: they give additional retrospective value to his life by their remembrances of him. So, in this way at least, meaning can be bestowed as well as imposed upon a man's life.

We have, then, a spectrum of opinions to consider. For some the meaning of my life is entirely my own creation. For others, I must bow to a fate written in the stars or in my genes. But the most reasonable view is an intermediate one. The purpose of my life is to be discovered through the interplay of two elements, the moral posture and policies I set out to face life with, and the suggestions life makes to me through my nature, my friends, and my circumstances. And the two interact. Persons with different attitudes *to* life perceive different meanings *in* life, so that moral orientation and perceived meaning are interdependent: change one, and the other changes. The ideal is to discover or create a reciprocal fit between them, so that imposed and perceived meanings make up a harmonious whole.[3] What I mean to do and what I am meant to do coincide. This ideal is expressed in the concept of *vocation*.

2 *Meaning as explanation and justification*

The second meaning of meaning is the solution of a problem. One notices a contrast between what R. W. Hepburn and John Wisdom have written about the meaning of life. When Hepburn ponders the meaning of life he thinks mainly of purpose and value. But when Wisdom ponders the meaning of life he thinks of an unsolved

[3] See H. H. Price, *Belief* (London, 1969), especially pp. 455-88. Price considers a world-view as a set of recommendations to view life in a certain way, act upon certain assumptions, and adopt certain policies: and then considers how far his consequent experience of life might verify the recommendations for someone who acts on them.

riddle, or a mystery which tantalizes us with the promise of a solution.[4]

In this way of thinking the meaning of a thing is its explanation —what has caused it, what its effects will be, and how it is to be interpreted.

The range of occasions embraced by this group of senses of meaning is very large. One can talk of the meaning of a religious ritual, or of an allegory, myth, parable, riddle, or conventional sign. The meaning is the thing signified. One may explain the meaning of some medical symptoms by citing the disease whose presence they indicate. The detective in a classical murder story is able to find significance in bizarre and fragmentary scraps of evidence through a flash of intuition by which he creates a bold explanatory hypothesis connecting them all plausibly together.

If I ask for the meaning of the latest news from China I am asking what underlies the news. I will be able to understand it if I am told what the present situation is, how it has arisen, and can guess the motives of those concerned and likely future developments. There is here an implicit ideal of explanation. A thing or event is explained by setting it in a context: the full story.[5] The search for meaning is the search for *dramatic* sense, and only when we are told the whole story, and are satisfied, does the item which puzzled us fall into place. We now know its meaning.

The relation between the puzzling thing or event and its meaning which we seek may be described as that of part to whole, surface to depth, manifest to latent, apparent to real, outside to inside, foreground to background, or text to interpretation.

And when someone explains a strange piece of conduct by revealing his real purpose we find explanation running into justification, autobiography into apologia. 'What is the meaning of this?' demands the voice of authority, requiring that the culprit shall at least attempt to justify conduct which is *prima facie* culpable.

So, in these cases, the search for intelligibility, the attempt to discern purpose, and the demand for vindication of what seems evil run very close together. In the quest for the meaning of life part of

[4] R. W. Hepburn, 'Questions about the Meaning of Life', *Religious Studies*, 1, pp. 125-40; John Wisdom, *Philosophy and Psychoanalysis* (Oxford, 1953), *passim*.
[5] There is an interesting use of 'story' in laboratory research work. The intermediate stage between first observing something odd and the formal published paper is called the 'story', and grasping the story is an essential stage in research work.

what we seek must be an explanation of all things which is the whole story. It will incorporate everything into a grand design, and in the unfolding of that design we hope to see apparent malignities and obscurities rectified and clarified. We seem to be asking that the nature of things shall be intelligible in terms of a purpose and moral agency resembling our own. It is as if the cosmic drama cannot be a drama for us except on our terms, on human terms, just as novels can only be written about animals or Martians by anthropomorphizing them.

Exception has been taken to the comprehensiveness of the phrase 'the meaning of life'. However, since it is quite reasonable to explain the meaning of a part by exhibiting its place in the whole, there is no logical objection to an inquiry after the *meaning* of all things, as there *is* a logical objection to the phrase, the *cause* of all things.

The moral demand in the search for meaning is well illustrated by a passage from *A Grief Observed*, by C. S. Lewis.[6] The writer is struggling to come to terms with the death of his wife. He tries to relate the fact and manner of her death to what he believes about God. There is an apparent moral contradiction. He considers (p. 28) the possibility that human moral judgement is so depraved that all its values are inverted. What we call evil, God calls good; what seems wrong and terrible to us seems right and proper to him. But if so, says Lewis, God is eradicated for all practical and speculative purposes. If God is not morally intelligible he is not knowable at all. The word good 'becomes meaningless' when applied to him. We can have no motive for obeying him. We can neglect even his power to enforce his promises and threats, because we can have no assurance that he will fulfil them. On such a view of things, says Lewis, 'reality at its very root' is 'meaningless to us'.

3 *Meaning as reality or substance*

In the third place we notice that meaning is spoken of in images of stuff, substance, weight, breadth, and reality. 'There's not an atom of meaning in it', declares Alice, as if meaning were material in a container. What has meaning is full, laden, and pregnant. What lacks meaning is empty, futile, and barren. What has meaning is useful, profitable, and worthwhile; what lacks it is useless, unprofitable, and worthless.

'Meaning' is often used to speak of direct first-hand experience

[6] Published as by N. W. Clerk (London, 1961); by C. S. Lewis (1964).

of the full reality of a thing. One may say, 'You don't know what poverty means, you've only imagined or read about it, you haven't actually experienced it, you don't know the meaning of poverty.'

Finally, we sometimes talk about what a thing means to us, by which we mean the sum of its influence upon us, its imaginative associations for us, our understanding of it. What a thing means to us is its reality *for us*. Highly complex entities like a religion, a city, a writer's work, or indeed a person may mean very different things to different people.

We have now briefly surveyed some of the relevant meanings of meaning.

We can think of meaning as purpose, as what a man means to do, and also as what he is meant to do: as a structure of purposings posited by him, or entered into and accepted by him, which collectively give his life worth.

We can think of meaning as explanation, as an answer to life's riddle, or a telling of the whole story of things which will finally satisfy us.

And we can think of meaning as reality, as an experience of life in which we are free of illusion, so that what we subjectively appropriate is nothing less than the full reality and truth of things as they really are.

Now it is striking that so many of the idioms in which we talk of the meaning of life carry a suggestion of ethical monotheism. But there are some reasons for caution here.

In the first place, our contemporary idioms also include many fossil remains of pagan theology, primitive science, and indeed superstition. I may say that my number is up, that I am in a sanguine humour, that the sun is setting, that a venture was ill-starred, that you are behaving like a man possessed, that a piece of music is martial, or a countenance saturnine. The idioms live on, but they no longer commit us to the belief-systems out of which they originally arose, any more than profanities commit us to belief in the deities invoked in them.

To this it may be replied that the idioms live on because they are useful, and say something needing to be said, but not easily said any other way. They enrich our response to the world. So that even though we have no intention of resuscitating the obsolete belief-systems which originally generated the idioms, we may still wish to keep as much as we can of the rich vocabulary of the meaning of life.

We may accept this point, as Hepburn does, but would agree with him that careful discrimination will be needed, and possibly considerable reinterpretation.

The second caveat is that the idioms in which we speak of the meaning of life are not wholly coherent. For example, some of the language has a Christian and some a pagan background. And it may be said that the demand for the whole story, a recounting of the cosmic drama in humanly intelligible terms, is a demand which it is impossible satisfactorily to meet.

> This world's no blot for us,
> Nor blank; it means intensely and means good:
> To find its meaning is my meat and drink.

In Browning's words the faith that the world means intensely and means good motivates the quest, but it does not amount to a claim to have found the meaning. It expresses only a faith that the meaning is to be found, and a determination to attempt to find it.

The idioms in which we speak of the meaning of life will therefore probably require more or less of expurgation and reinterpretation. Just how much is controversial. The atheistic existentialists take an extreme view by rejecting all such talk out of hand. Richard Robinson, in his book *An Atheist's Values*,[7] is nearly as radical. For him the wise man is the man who judges some finite thing or state of affairs to be good and attainable, and achieves it. There is nothing to be gained and everything to be lost by dreaming of an absolute good. Talk of the meaning of life, or of an ultimate end of all action, is not only mystifying but pernicious, for it leads us to depreciate goods near at hand, and robs us of our appetite for this our only life. So Robinson rejects almost the entire vocabulary of the meaning of life as otiose and harmful.

In their papers on this subject Kurt Baier, Kai Nielson and Anthony Flew have taken a nearly similar view.[8] A man's life is meaningful if he pursues valuable ends. Only he can judge them to be valuable, so that it is up to the man himself to give his own life

[7] Oxford, 1964.
[8] These papers are discussed in R. W. Hepburn's article cited above. See also Karl Britton, *Philosophy and the Meaning of Life* (Cambridge, 1969).

meaning. A god cannot do it for him. The suggestion that a man may be the instrument through which some larger purpose is executed is incompatible with moral autonomy. There is not and cannot be some esoteric wisdom which is the meaning of life.

A slightly different view is taken by the young Bertrand Russell, especially in the letters to G. L. Dickinson written between 1902 and 1904.[9] Russell affirms that 'the unmystical rationalistic view of life seems to me to omit all that is most important and most beautiful': but, as always, he sharply distinguishes the provinces of Science and Mysticism. Mysticism discovers no fresh truth; rather it 'creates the truth it believes in, by the way in which it feels the fundamental facts—the helplessness of man before Time and Death, and the strange depths of feeling which lie dormant until some one of the Gods of life calls for our worship. Religion and art both, it seems to me, are attempts to humanise the universe', they are at best affirmations that 'although man may be powerless, his ideals are not so'.

Thus Russell professes to value highly religious feeling and a religious response to the world. But it is not cognitive. In the end we are 'the plaything of vast irresistible irrational forces' from which there is no escape.

Russell's position seems to me mistaken. Our feeling-response to things may be appropriate and reasonable or inappropriate and unreasonable. It is reasonable to love the lovely, hate the hateful, worship the worshipful. But feelings may be unreasonable, too. In a mild case of inappropriate feeling-response we may ask, 'Why are you so cheerful?' In an acute case we speak of serious emotional disorder. It is unreasonable to continue to respond emotionally to the world as if some religion were true while expressly denying that any religion is true. Religious attitudes are propositional and in so far as they really *are* found to be apt and fitting we have surely some reason to think the propositions true.

Hepburn follows Russell in valuing some aspects of the religious response to the world. Against such as Flew and Nielsen he defends the notion of a single unifying purpose in life. For we can go beyond a simple plurality of purposes and point to the way in which, for example, a great love may unify a life.

But he is aware of how much difference theism makes, and that in two dimensions. First, on the humanist view, the larger the frame

[9] Reprinted in Volume I of Russell's *Autobiography* (London, 1967), pp. 185-9.

of reference, or the more distant the standpoint from which human life is contemplated, the more it is dwarfed and reduced to a petty disturbance on the satellite of a minor star at the fringe of a galaxy. The theist does not suffer this sense of diminishment. Secondly, on the theistic view our life is enacted against the vast backdrop of eternity. Pilgrimage here, arrival there: affliction here, reward and recompense there. Take away the backdrop and you are left with a sense of life in which there is too much of preparation and too little of achievement.

Hepburn feels that the humanist's sense of life must on any showing have much of the tragic about it. Yet a man's life may exhibit a unity, something like the unity of a piece of discourse;[10] and indeed one of the noblest of literary forms, biography, expresses the unity of a life in a piece of discourse. 'To contemplate the web of one's life's aims, its themes and articulating images' may afford as much fulfilment of the longing for eternity as is to be had. Life begins with one cry and ends with another, and what comes between, when pondered, may disclose a shape and a meaning of which we are glad.

But still Hepburn leaves out what is *given*. He acknowledges that I may discover that I am unfitted for a certain course of life, but does not attend to what it is to find out what one is really fitted for. One must distinguish between the life a man has and the life he leads. If I say that John makes life hard for himself, or that he has led a pretty meaningless life, then that is his *fault*. Whereas if I say that John has had a hard life, or that life has been hard on John, then that is his *misfortune*, not his fault. There may be a broad proportion between the measure we mete and the measure we get, but they are distinct. There is the meaning we posit or put into life, and the meaning we find or receive.

My life is the product of my engagement during its course with what is not myself. We have to think not only of what a man means in his life but also of the ranges of meaning disclosed to a man by his life-experience. In artistic creation, in faith, in the quest for meaning there is a subtle dialectical relation between the meaning and reality which we posit and that which we apprehend. Indeed the ambiguity between what is perceived and what is posited by us is contained within the range of use of such words as invention and discovery, and creates classical controversies within the philosophies of mathematics, of art, and of science. Does the mind create and impose order, or perceive and trace it? I think both, as indeed

[10] See I. Dilman's paper in *Religious Studies*, 3, pp. 547ff.

our ordinary language suggests. The meaning of our lives is something to be willed and achieved, and something to be discerned: something to be fulfilled by us, and in us. And the meaning we affirm somehow evokes the meaning we discern. We are no more likely to capture this in a single forever-definitive form of words than to see it expressed in a single definitive work of art. A bony, angular myth, endlessly suggestive and capable of various interpretations, may be of more use.

So much for the meaning of life. The purpose of this analysis has been to introduce an old religious principle which is highly relevant to our theme. It is that the measure you mete is the measure you receive: the moral orientation and interpretative framework with which you approach life decides what meaning you will perceive *in* life: the programme you set out with decides the results you will obtain.

In the computer world they have a saying, 'Garbage in, garbage out'. The results you obtain are a function of, and can be no better than, the programme you put into the machine. It is a modern version of the Gospel saying that the measure you mete is the measure you get, the way you search determines what you will find.

Now there is a hopeful and interesting analogy here. We began with contemporary worries about pluralism and relativism. Pluralism seemed to be at once an important and morally valuable intellectual achievement, and at the same time a threat to reason and the unity of truth. Each item of our knowledge and belief seemed relative to the interpretative framework and set of assumptions through which it was obtained; and there appeared to be no independent standpoint from which, or criteria by which, it could be appraised. Is our culture under the threat of disintegration into a host of rival and incompatible ideologies or 'programmes', which admit of no independent rational appraisal?

Now we find that something very similar has long been recognized in religion. The only way to the truth in religion is by a confession of ignorance, through an admission of the relativity even of the central religious doctrines and images. Here is a clue, but the way forward will not be easy.

5

Patterns and Facts

We now have to develop the notion of a programme, both in secular and religious contexts.

In recent years experimental psychologists have studied intensively the way in which we learn to see, and to recognize objects.[1] It seems that from the very beginning of our lives our brains are busily at work constructing a complex hypothesis as to what the world about us is like. There is an overall world-picture, and an exceedingly large stock of patterns, and rules connecting patterns with objects. Only pause for a moment, and consider, first, how many diverse things we instantly recognize for hats; and secondly, how many even more diverse visual presentations are instantly interpreted by us as occasions of seeing these same hats.

The conclusions which have been reached can be conveyed by describing an attempt to copy human object-recognition by using a computer with a television input. The computer has to be programmed with a description of the object, say a pair of spectacles. This description has to be sufficiently general to allow for a certain range of variation in frame design, for the possibility that the sides may be folded or unfolded, and for the different images the object presents when seen from different points of view. The complete programme is thus rather complicated. The computer is programmed in this way for about a dozen objects. When one of them is set before the television camera the computer then scans the pattern presented to it on the screen, and begins to search its memory for something corresponding to the presented image. Even a rather powerful computer takes about ten minutes to perform this trivially simple task which we are able to perform in an immeasurably brief time.

That we do see the world about us in this way is, nevertheless, evident to the layman's introspection. Suppose you are searching your bookshelves for your copy of *Anna Karenina*. It seems certain

[1] See, for example, Richard Gregory, *Eye and Brain* (2nd edn., London, 1972); *The Intelligent Eye* (London, 1970).

that when we look for something we fix our minds upon a mental picture of the thing we are looking for, and then scan the environment looking for an object which matches this picture. So, in looking for *Anna Karenina*, you first try to recall what your copy looks like. You ask yourself whether it is hardback or paperback; whether old or new; whether the dominant colour is red, navy blue, or whatever; and whether the title runs horizontally across, or vertically down, the spine. Having decided that your *Anna Karenina* is a shabby red and white Penguin with a vertical title, you begin to scan the shelves. If your memory is detailed and correct your mental picture will soon meet its match, and you will pick out the volume. But if your programming is misleading it will conceal the volume from you, and you may fail to find it even after repeated searches. I find also that it is very difficult to scan in this way for more than one volume at once. It is quicker to look for two or three titles successively rather than simultaneously.

This is a very simple example of a programme, deliberately adopted to aid the performance of an elementary task. The programme is *a posteriori*: it is a visual memory, though we should remember that whether or not visual memories take the form of mental images is a matter of controversy among psychologists. It is because their visual memories are less well stocked than those of adults, and their hypotheses about the world less highly developed, that children are so notoriously bad at looking for things. They are not able to make good guesses about where a thing is likely to be, nor do they have detailed enough visual memories to suggest good hypotheses about the appearances it may present to the searching eye. But they have a corresponding advantage: just because they are less good at looking for things they are much better at noticing things. Their gaze upon the world is less specialized and selective. Walking by a canal once with a child I recognized something as a dragonfly, an *Aeshna*; but he, who did not recognize it, was the first to notice it fly backwards.

This does make clear some of the advantages and disadvantages of a highly trained mind. To get far in any science one must acquire highly complex mental programming, programming which may make one efficient, but second-rate. Only the best minds can achieve a thorough grasp of the conceptual framework of their science while yet retaining a child's flexibility of attention and ability to notice the unexpected. Such people, who have kept the child's mind, can avoid being blinded by their own mental programming. They can tell when it becomes obstructive, discard it, and perhaps try out another model. Indeed, in some of the most highly developed sciences, in particular physics, the knack of moving about among various models has actually become incorporated into the structure of the science: another analogy between modern physics and classical theology.

Since many experimental psychologists are behaviourists I should say that for the purposes of the argument of this book a purely behaviouristic interpretation of hypothesis framing and testing is insufficient and unacceptable. Let me bring out the difference which consciousness makes, by describing an experiment.

The subject is seated before a screen on which are displayed a number of digits, at first 000. As he sits there the number begins to rise slowly: 001, 002. He is promised a handsome reward if he can make the number rise more rapidly, but he is given no instructions as to how to make this happen. Nevertheless, after a few moments the number begins to rise with gradually accelerating rapidity. After three or four minutes, the number is in the hundreds, but when the experiment stops, the subject has no idea how he has done it. He has, perhaps, unconsciously tried out various hypotheses: he has certainly unconsciously learned to perform his allotted task. But though there has been hypothesis framing and testing, and though there has been learning, he still does not realize that in fact he was being rewarded for blinking.

Now it seems to me intuitively evident that there is a great deal of difference between the ability to learn unconsciously, which was demonstrated by this experiment, and conscious learning. The behaviourist cannot to my mind do sufficient justice to this vast difference, a difference which is often obscured by careless talk about chromosomes carrying 'information', or about flatworms 'learning'. Our own interest is in occasions where we become *conscious* of our own thinking, our own programming, and so conscious of its limits. We transcend ourselves for a moment in that act. But it is an act of *consciousness*, of spirit.

Another philosophical point needs to be made. The modern discovery of the elaborate and various mental programmes with which we address ourselves to the world, and by which we interpret it, seems to be related to the philosophy of Kant. For Kant above all insisted that all our objective empirical knowledge is formed by the application to sense intuitions of a whole arsenal of interpretative concepts. However, Kant's method of transcendental proof

was *a priori*. He hoped to demonstrate *a priori* that only one programme was possible: one particular programme was supposed to
be demonstrably the necessary condition of the possibility of objective knowledge of the phenomenal world.

Now we have an odd antinomy, for what Kant purports to prove
a priori is at variance with the results of empirical enquiry. For
example, Kant says we see the world, and must see it, as a system
of objects moving about in Euclidean space. But this is empirically
untrue. We do not see geometrical perspective. A mechanism known
as 'constancy scaling' ensures that though remote objects are seen
as distant, they are not seen as being so small as the laws of geometrical perspective require. What is more, men do demonstrably
differ in their perception of space, for optical illusion-figures affect
people from different cultures differently. Forest peoples, who are
unused to seeing a long way, and Zulus, whose traditional culture
gives them little experience of straight lines and right angles, have
a demonstrably different experience of space from Westerners. And
it is well known that in different artistic traditions distance is represented in different ways.

In fact, Euclidean space and geometrical perspective are not
universal and absolute, but are cultural creations, the former of
ancient Greece, and the latter of Renaissance Italy. So there has been
a great change since Kant's day. He recognized that our empirical
knowledge is relative to intellectual programming, but thought he
could vindicate the objectivity of knowledge by proving *a priori*
that there is and can be only one programme. But we know empirically that there is an endless variety of different programmes.
Different men have looked and do look at the world in different
ways, and see different things.

How far does the relativity of programmes extend? Suppose we
agree to consider the human brain as a computer. There is a continuous input into the machine, and the machine is continuously
searching its input for recurring patterns, and constructing and testing hypotheses. The machine thus gradually builds up a world-
picture, and gradually becomes more efficient at interpreting its input
promptly. If this is how the mind works, then the different inputs in
different human societies and environments will lead to the formation
of different world-pictures.

But the actual human situation is enormously more complex even
than this. Men are, or may be, conscious; they are agents; and they
influence each other. And it is a fact of experience that, if the

flourishing of human groups inspired by them is any criterion, efficient action-guiding belief-systems may be endlessly diverse and even self-confirming. This applies not only to mythology, to religion, or to ethics, but also to science. We may think the diversity of successful cults in California hard for a rationalist to stomach, but so is the coexistence of anaesthetics with acupuncture in China, and of Western psychiatry with witch-doctoring in Africa.

I shall use the phrase 'the interpretative plasticity of the world' to describe the curious way in which the world of our experience is seemingly willing to lend itself to interpretation in terms of a great variety of different programmes. I reiterate that this is a matter of daily experience in a pluralistic society, something people joke about when they compile a comic symposium interpreting *Winnie the Pooh* or *Alice in Wonderland* from a wide variety of ideological standpoints. The world not only lends itself to these varied interpretations, it actually seems, in the eyes of believers at least, to ratify each of them with equal generosity. Our task is to reconcile this fact of life with belief in reason and in God.

Before we move on, let us develop this theme with a few examples.

1. One of the most important entirely non-Western cultures surviving (precariously) in the modern world is that of Japan. Encountering it, one learns how deep cultural differences can be. A Westerner in the audience finds a Noh play very hard to understand, for three reasons: the system of values embodied in the play is not his own; the way people respond emotionally in various situations is different; and some of the emotions are linked to facial expressions different from those to which he is accustomed. A Westerner's bafflement at a Noh play is instructive, because it shows him that, however open-minded he fancies himself to be, he does in fact bring to theatrical experience a great body of internal programming. He does not bring to a play a mind which is a blank slate. On the contrary, he brings to it the expectations of an entire culture; and when the play does not fit those expectations he is baffled.

2. It is said that the Tractarian John Keble, when vicar of a country parish, used deliberately to preach boring sermons so that people should not think him clever. He did it as an exercise in humility. Now, leaving aside the question whether Keble was right to act this way, let us ask how could anyone guess what he was doing? After all, boring sermons are not uncommon, but members

of congregations seldom surmise that the preacher is cultivating the virtue of humility. To guess what Keble was up to, it seems, one would need to understand something of the Tractarian moral universe, of the importance of the concept of humility in it, and of the (perhaps rather dotty) things a man might be led to do in the pursuit of this virtue. Indeed, I suggest that you would need to have felt the influence of these Tractarian evaluations, in order to see why the role of applauded popular preacher would be repellent to Keble, why he would instinctively prefer to be earnest and commonplace rather than showy. Keble's dull sermons would sift his hearers; those whose religion was superficial would go away complaining loudly and not return, and those who were morally serious about their religion would stay. At any rate it is clear that what a person made of Keble's preaching would be the outcome of the interaction of two things—the objective content and delivery of the sermon, and the moral experience and opinions of the hearer himself.

The making of moral judgements is impossible without moral programming. No moral judgement can be made about a man unless the observer applies moral concepts to the observed behaviour: and no correct moral judgement can be made unless the observer and the one observed *share* a good many moral concepts.

3. The debate between egoists and altruists shows clearly the link between preconceptions and perceptions. If you side with the egoists, and in your psychology go along with Bentham, Freud, or the early Sartre, you will be sceptical about what may seem at first sight to be instances of truly disinterested conduct, and perhaps become adept at explaining them away. If on the other hand you do believe in the possibility of disinterested conduct, you will soon find yourself observing instances of it. The differences between the various schools of psychology—between stimulus-response theorists, psychoanalysts, depth-psychologists, differential psychologists, personalists, cognitive theorists, and so on—are largely programmatic differences; that is, differences in philosophy of life, in beliefs about what men are and in what terms human behaviour should be explained.

4. The principle that what you believe determines what you can see does not apply solely to the realm of personal relationships, or the perception of moral truths. For example, Charles Darwin's main theses in *The Origin of Species* are, I believe, substantially correct. By that I mean that a Darwinian explanation of, for

example, the fossil record, is nearer the mark than the explanations offered by seventeenth-century biologists. I am not arguing for scepticism about scientific theories. Nevertheless the truth is that the way Darwin saw biological evolution was influenced by contemporary moral and political ideas and facts. He saw the individual organism struggling for survival in an environment teeming with rivals; he saw the strong prevailing over the weak; he saw progress through competition; he saw some whose natural endowments favoured their survival and others whose natural disadvantages meant inevitable defeat: and he saw these things because the culture he lived in taught him to look out for them. He did not like them, but Malthus and others had persuaded him that they were facts.[2]

It would have been possible, with a different set of initial expectations, for Darwin to have arrived at a very different version of evolutionary theory. He might, for example, have believed in a holistic approach, and in the corporate state. Instead of beginning with the individual, one might begin with the entire system of living things which occupies a particular habitat—an ecosystem. The story of evolution then becomes the story of how the ecosystem differentiates itself internally so as to fill the habitat with as rich and diverse a tapestry of life as possible, within the limits set by such factors as the availability of solar energy, water, and the various essential elements. The richer and more varied the ecosystem the better its chances of adapting to large-scale and long-term climatic and geological changes, because it has more internal variety to draw on.

Darwin's story, broadly speaking, reflected the Protestant ethic, *laissez-faire*, and the spirit of capitalism. Mine reflects, broadly speaking, a more collectivist ethic. Each seems to be a possible way of presenting evolutionary ideas. What you 'see' in nature seems to depend, at least partly, on the moral opinions which you hold, and which you expect to see nature echo.

We must add briefly here that modern psychology has confirmed what is a matter of everyday observation, that the simplest sense-perception is a socially learned skill, acquired with much effort. I have lately been teaching my young children bird-recognition, and the use of magnifying lenses. I was astonished that they could not

[2] This has been spelt out in a number of papers by R. M. Young: e.g. 'Malthus and the Evolutionists', *Past and Present*, no. 43 (May 1969), pp. 109-41.

see through the instrument even quite simple structures disclosed by it unless I first drew the thing to look for, and they then looked and recognized it, because I had naively forgotten the years I spent myself as a schoolboy learning to see things through a microscope. How difficult it is to see something accurately without the guidance of someone who has seen it before and can tell one what to look for! Such historical cases as the homunculus, or the canals on Mars, remind one of the striking extent to which one observes what one expects to see. One almost suspects that no single individual, but only a consensus of observers, can make an entirely fresh observation.[3]

5. Nor does the application of our principle extend only to the biological sciences. Much of the history of physics reveals a conviction that permanent unchanging principles underlie the flux of appearances. They are there to be discovered, and there is a duty to find them. One is struck by Newton's resolve to make the solar system stable, and resort to any expedient, however implausible, to eliminate the threat of imbalance; and one suspects that the advocates of the 'steady state' theory in recent years were motivated by a similar desire. Physicists do not sit back and wait for the world to show its order: they set out to put it into order, with considerable determination. Seventeenth-century science, in love with mathematics, sought immutable laws of nature, and self-evident truths of reason. Finding them (as they thought), men came to believe also in an immutable natural moral law, and inalienable moral rights. The world-view of classical physics led to the politics of Tom Paine, and the American and French Revolutions. Hume connected atomism in natural philosophy with an atomistic theory of knowledge; Kant, in his *Dreams of a Spirit-Seer*, carried ideas of attraction and repulsion over from physics to ethics. There were affinities between atomism in physics and bourgeois individualism. So we may look at it the other way round, and begin instead with Hooker and Grotius, with the emergence of bourgeois capitalism, and with the Amsterdam of the early seventeenth century. From this perspective we see the social facts creating the scientific theories, rather than the other way round. Put the two together, and we see classical physics and classical liberal republicanism growing

[3] An outstanding example is the utter bewilderment of Galileo and Huygens, when they first saw Saturn through telescopes. Previous astronomical experience had not given them any object-hypothesis through which they could recognize what they saw. Indeed, they could not *see* what was before their eyes.

together and influencing each other. And the new scientific world-view, assiduously propagated, does its job of confirming the growing authority of men of science as effectively as the old religious world-views had confirmed the authority of the priests.

6. In all, or at any rate much, of our knowledge, it seems, we scan the world looking for patterns which fit our own preconceptions. Sometimes the results are comical: for example, men have been speculating for three centuries about the original purpose and use of the great monument at Stonehenge, and their speculations have been ludicrously revealing of the fantasies of their authors' own periods. The latest fads have been to describe Stonehenge as a 'computer', or an astronomical observatory, or both, but these are only the latest in a long series of equally improbable theories. The quest of the historical Shakespeare is another example: with un-failing regularity each writer has demonstrated that Shakespeare was an idealized version of himself. Searching for Shakespeare, one looks into a mirror.

It seems, then, that we are obliged to admit that the human mind can address itself to the world in a variety of different ways, with different internal programmes, and that the world accordingly yields up different messages to different men. In any particular epoch and place there is of course a mainstream of assumptions shared by most of the ablest and most active men, but this body of culturally dominant assumptions is itself in continuous change.

These considerations change the shape of our task. People have proclaimed the cultural relativity of ethics and of religion, as if these admitted facts did not apply to science as well. They have urged that in matters of ethics and religion we are inevitably biased by our preconceptions, as if the same did not apply to science as well. But it does.

Yet is not a religious attitude to the world particularly 'subjective'? Are we not, in the case of religion, particularly liable to deception by our own unconscious fantasies? I have to stress this point because I am not a sceptic about science. I acknowledge the cultural rela-tivity of Darwin's own Darwinism, yet still think he gives basically the correct answers to questions about, for example, what fossils are, and how they got where they are. But in the case of alleged religious knowledge, does *anything* remain after we have made due allowance for cultural relativity and subjective distortion?

RELIGIOUS ATTITUDES AND RELIGIOUS TRUTHS

When a man joins a religious community he wants to learn, embrace, and make habitual a certain set of mind and a certain way of life. He has tried them on in imagination, and found he likes the feel of them. He feels certain that there is here for him a prospect of sure spiritual development—growth in understanding, moral progress, and, most important of all, a proper pattern of response to the awesome quasi-erotic attraction of the sacred.

This body of material he wants to appropriate contains, as we see by now, a variety of elements:

1 He accepts that some object or goal is of supreme worth, so that all his life ought to be oriented towards it.

2 He accepts that the community's law is the right path by which to attain it.

3 He accepts, or intends to learn and accept, a philosophy of life: a broad characterization of the human situation in view of which it is clear that a life lived by the community's law, and in its membership, is the good life, and the best life for a man to live.

4 He thus gains a value-system, confirmed by the community's traditions, and exemplified in its saints.

5 As he sinks into his new life, the world increasingly lends itself to his new way of looking at it, and his faith grows stronger. His new life-style is increasingly self-verifying. He grows in religious knowledge.

6 He learns to understand and articulate his own version of the community's belief-system. The system of doctrinal beliefs expresses the objective correlate of his new way of life.

A few people are first attracted by the objective side of religion: the doctrines, the philosophy of life, and the value-system appeal to them as answering certain problems. Young Prince Gautama, it is said, was brought up to a life of ease, and first awoke spiritually when he saw successively an ageing man, a diseased man, and a corpse. His religious awakening was brought about by the questions these sights prompted. Final happiness cannot be had in the world of sense if age, sickness, and death always at last prevail in it.

But most people, probably, are first drawn towards the subjective side of religion. They are attracted to the faith by which others believe, rather than the faith in which they believe. So, in the same narrative of the Buddha Shakyamuni's earthly life, other people are captivated by the spiritual virtues of holy men. They are struck with admiration for these men, and desire to emulate their virtues by becoming their disciples. Only at a later stage do they make the doctrines their own too. The Buddha himself could not take this route, because of course there could be no one superior to himself whose disciple he might become; but even he needed the sight of a mendicant to prompt him to remember his destined vocation.

The two sides of religion, doctrine and piety, clearly correspond to each other. The sort of piety one embraces decides the sort of doctrines at which one will eventually arrive. Different initial religious postures will lead on to different ultimate religious truths.

We now see looming towards us the central problem. A man drawn to Buddhism is attracted by a certain style of piety, way of thinking, and cluster of virtues. Appropriating these, he hopes to set out on the way to knowledge. But they have already determined where his quest will lead him. Adopt this programme, this way of looking at things, and you will be led at last to a vision of the universe in which there is no place for a personal god. The truths which his religious quest will finally disclose to him were implicit from the start. Embrace this morality, these techniques of meditation, this way of life, and the truths disclosed to you will be such and such.

Conversely, suppose a man attracted to Christianity. Its piety proposes a different notion of prayer; not a trance in which the self disappears, but active struggle to conform oneself to the divine will. And the virtues are different: active love for one's individual fellow-man is not a minor virtue or a side-shoot of the spiritual life, but stands at the head of the list. The divine is approached through response to the claims of a fellow-man. And again, the initial set of attitudes one appropriates surely predetermines the answers at which the religious quest will eventually arrive.

We have seen already that it is a principle of wide application that the patterns in one's mind decide the truths one will be able to perceive. It seems particularly applicable to religions, which seem to be internally verified complexes of ideas and practices. Piety shapes doctrine, and doctrine confirms piety.

We may attempt to avoid the difficulty by abstracting the doctrines of a religion and subjecting them to independent philosophical analysis and criticism. Belief in God, for example, may be so treated. The results are very disappointing. Torn from its proper context, the belief becomes unrecognizable. But in its proper context, it seems uncriticizable.

We are faced again with what I have called 'the interpretative plasticity of the world' and of human nature: that is, the curious way in which the world in general, and human nature in particular, accommodate themselves to an extraordinary[4] variety of interpretations. A comparative anthropologist, considering the variety of human cultures and mythologies, may notice this; so may the historian of comparative religion; so may the student of the history of metaphysics in China, India and the West; and so may the observer of the variety of ideologies current in a modern pluralistic society. How does it come about that the world and human nature are so plastic, so readily accommodate themselves to such a bewildering variety of interpretative frameworks?[5] A religion, a powerful ideology, a metaphysical system, seem each to be complete universes. And I have been saying that we may be deluding ourselves if we fancy that we can take up a neutral and unbiased standpoint from which we can survey the varieties of dogmatic folly.

It is, for example, idle to pretend at this time of day that the world-view of natural science offers any such standpoint; for there are some clearly identifiable presuppositions of the scientific enterprise which predetermine the character of the results at which it arrives. One is that man in thought alienates himself from nature and considers it (and even himself as part of it) as from outside with complete objectivity. The second, related to it, is that his only moral imperative is to be thus objective, and admit no other moral considerations. Other presuppositions define what shall count as 'scientific' ways of describing, classifying, analysing, and explaining phenomena. The result of beginning from these presuppositions is of course the creation of a vast body of knowledge and considerable technical power—but with no ethical directives, and an uneasy sense of alienation: an outcome which may yet destroy us all. And the initial postulates of method were, admittedly,

[4] Since there is only one world for us to know, there is a logical difficulty about calling any general feature of it 'extraordinary'. I mean, extraordinary by the standards of earlier periods when men were less aware than we of the world's interpretative plasticity.

[5] An example which impressed me is this: The culture of the Australian aborigines seems very strange to Westerners. Yet the Australian aborigine was so well adapted to his environment that in his hey-day, before the white man came, he could make the Australian outback support more people per square mile than the white man has been able to yet.

arbitrary. They cannot be proved from any body of scientific knowledge prior to them, because any body of scientific knowledge must
presuppose them to merit the name.

But if scientific knowledge is thus relative to certain assumptions,
and it is demonstrable that these assumptions have potentially exceedingly damaging consequences, we must clearly keep open
the possibility that other assumptions, other ways of relating ourselves cognitively to the world, may yield better results.

It seems then that, in a culture like our own, one is almost free
to choose what the world shall be like; free to create the world in
thought, and make of it what one will. In classical Greek and Christian thought the world of nature was, for many centuries, thought
of as a fully constituted system, with a determinate, stable structure.
God finished the stage, and then put men on it. But the drift of
modern thought has been away from this idea. The world is not
finished, so that the human mind has nothing more to do than to
accommodate itself to a world-order already settled and complete
before the human mind appears on the scene.[6] Rather, the process
of creation is completed only by human thought and action. A
plastic world interacts with various human interpretative frameworks to gain a finished shape, or rather, a variety of possible
finished shapes. The history of thought in a particular culture
is a history of an ongoing interaction between changing interpretative
frameworks and the various world-pictures which these frameworks
yield as they are applied to experience. The mind which scans
the world, and the meanings which the world delivers up to the
mind, are both changing all the time. The old dream of permanent
and perspicuous knowledge of unchangeable real objects seems
nowadays a mirage; and one who ponders the relation of thought
to reality is haunted constantly by the spectre of relativism.

Relativism has the effect of making us oscillate between dogmatism and scepticism. I am a dogmatist when I assert that I must
take my present interpretative framework on trust. It cannot itself
be justified: it can only be employed.[7] Unlike Kant, I cannot stave
off scepticism by pretending to prove *a priori* that it is the only

[6] Theology has already begun to make the change: for theologians have
come to speak of creation not as an act completed long ago, but as still
in process, and not complete until the end of the world. In the older theology
the old creation and the new were two distinct acts of God, one at the
beginning, the other at the end of time. Now they, and the idea of Providence, are all amalgamated in the one ongoing cosmic process.

[7] See R. G. Collingwood's *Essay on Metaphysics* (Oxford, 1940).

possible interpretative framework. I know perfectly well that others are possible. But then I realize that every item of objective knowledge is only knowledge relative to the interpretative framework through which it was obtained. There is no absolute knowledge, no item of knowledge which can be proved completely. And so I fall into scepticism.

How can a religious way to knowledge escape this trap? It does so through the idea of the transcendent, which alone is able to relativize and so overcome relativism itself. As our prison analogy in Chapter 3 made clear, it is not necessary to claim any direct intuition of transcendent reality: the prisoner did not find a peep-hole in the prison wall. Nor was it necessary to claim to possess a body of information about transcendent reality: the prisoner acknowledged how tenuous and insubstantial was anything he could say by the ways of negation, eminence, causality, and analogy. Rather, he was able to overcome relativity in thought, by understanding it. He saw the way in which language and thought within the prison were moulded by the state of imprisonment, and ratified it. People had become institutionally trapped by their very ways of thinking and speaking. They were caught in an enchanted sleep. Our man saw the way in which the prisoners' framework had become adapted to the little world in which they used it and so had become a cage which prevented them from awakening and realizing where they were. The idea of the transcendent came to our prisoner in a kind of ecstasy: for a moment he stood outside himself. In imagination he joined us who were thinking about his situation. He saw the world and its ways of thinking for a moment from outside, and as a whole.

'Everything flows', and religion begins precisely with an attempt to transcend the flux of things in thought. For when I think 'Everything flows', for a moment I transcend the flux. My life hitherto has been sunk in a monotonous routine from which I have not before now thought to raise my head: the moment I do, I have begun to break free. I have become conscious spirit. The sense of pervading relativity, the realization that I do not really know anything at all, my whole effort in life has achieved nothing—this is not the end, but the beginning. Just as I was sinking into scepticism I realize that the entertaining of the idea of a general scepticism is my first aspiration after the transcendent, after that which eludes head-on thinking, but is always behind me, just out of direct view. It is as when one trembles on the brink and then realizes that to be on the brink is, after all, to have firm ground behind one. To be able to see that everything flows is for a moment to have gained the bank, to view the world of change from a standpoint outside it which does not change. Change itself is unthinkable unless in thought we can for a moment compare it with an unchanging background against which it stands out clearly.

What we call the problem of relativism is simply a modern epistemologically minded way of speaking about what in earlier days was called the transience, or the corruptibility of things. To see that all things are corruptible is for a moment to imagine something incorruptible before which their changes show up clearly. To say 'All our knowledge is relative to interpretative frameworks' is to say something which, if true, *must be an exception to the rule it states*: to have been for a moment able to transcend our ordinary level and way of knowing and say something about it as a whole.

So religion aspires after absolute knowledge, while yet it recognizes that our situation is such that absolute knowledge is not attainable. Our age replies to this that all our knowledge is relative to interpretative frameworks: that there is no escape from relativity: and that religion above all is manifestly relative to certain social facts. My reply has been to disclaim any direct intuition of the absolute, and instead to point out that the statement 'All our knowledge is relative to interpretative frameworks', if something we know for true, is an exception to the rule it states. Precisely because we can grasp what relativism is and asserts, we can transcend it. The thing is proved possible by the fact that it is done; for example when we understand, find inadequate, and modify an interpretative framework which we have used unquestioningly hitherto. The idea of transcendence, in this very general sense, is necessary for creative advance in any department of human life and thought whatever.

But only the *idea* of transcendence has been vindicated so far, and here we must leave our analogy of the prisoner far behind. To understand the history of ideas, and the possibility of conceptual revolution and of growth in the moral life, we need to see how the idea of transcendence must be invoked. But can we turn about and face it directly? How about the *fact* of the transcendent? Religion does not deal with the idea of the transcendent merely as a necessary gymnastic trick for original thinkers or penitents: it goes on to propose that we orient our whole lives about the reality of the transcendent, and claims supreme importance in human life for the endeavour to do this.

And what of the paradox that religion, which professes to be concerned with the eternal, is as obviously culturally relative as any other human activity? This need not long detain us. All religions say that there are many nominal but only a few true believers; that most stop at the letter and only a few grasp the spirit. Since religion proposes to affect us more intimately and comprehensively than mathematics it is hardly surprising that the doctrines, images, rites, and rules of it should be more obviously culture-bound than is mathematics. As we shall see, there is indeed a level at which religion is clearly culture-bound: but we also intend to show that there is a level at which it transcends cultural relativity altogether.

6

Religious Knowledge

There is, we have been arguing, a continuously changing relationship between the interpretative frameworks with which we scan the world, and the meanings which the world so scanned delivers up to our thought. Framework M^1 discloses world-structure W^1, M^2 discloses W^2, and so on. Through the idea of the transcendent I am able to think (M^1W^1) as a single whole, and so move on in imagination to enter and compare a variety of different world-views.[1] With a considerable effort I can learn to see a falling body as Aristotle saw it, or see the sun and moon as an African tribesman saw them. Creative advance in human thought occurs when a thinker is conscious of considerable internal stresses within his world-picture, thinks it as a whole (M^2W^2), and is able to shift it, coming down again in (M^3W^3) which he judges to make a more satisfactory whole. He has skipped like a hermit crab from one shell to another. Something like this was achieved, by stages, between Copernicus and Newton, and between Malthus and Darwin.

An ecstasy, a standing-outside one's habitual ways of thinking, is involved here, and I have followed Kierkegaard in relating it to humour. If one thing is clear about the difference between the human mind and a machine, it is that machines lack the idea of the transcendent and so cannot invent jokes against themselves. It is conceivable that computers may be more flexible in their operation, that their problem-solving ability may be improved, and even that they may be taught how to make discoveries—but all this would be of a different order from the faculty I have been describing.

Religion's interpretative framework includes, of course, not only concepts and the skill of using them, but also a moral orientation. And, as we have said, the transcendent is for it more than a gymnas-

[1] Here and hereafter (M^xW^x) is used to stand for 'a conceptual scheme or interpretative framework, and the knowledge of the world which it yields as it is applied to experience; the two being considered together as a single whole, a way of thinking, a world-view'. Where I use an ordinal number in place of the 'x', as in (M^1W^1), I mean one particular such programme and body of knowledge.

tic device. It is the central focus of an entire life, an actual absolute good which harnesses all our energies and aspirations.[2]

Yet direct acquaintance with the transcendent is ruled out, not only by the terms of our earlier prison metaphor, and not only by the philosophical arguments against it, but by the actual language and teachings of the religions. The supreme object of religious aspiration is held to be ineffable and incomprehensible. The first principle of religious knowledge is the mysteriousness of its object: one knows by unknowing, is rich in poverty and full in emptiness, gains by losing, lives by dying.

This principle we shall in due course explore. But its immediate consequence is that we cannot explain religious knowledge by a crisp analysis of the absolute object known and the means by which it is known. That cannot be had, and to pretend otherwise would be idle, and indeed impious.

Instead we find that religious knowledge has a rather rich and cloudy structure. As there are many different sorts of knowing, and religion is the most all-inclusive of human activities, so all the different sorts of knowing enter into religious knowledge.

If a man is to be properly described as a proficient in religion he must possess at least the following:

1 *Descriptive knowledge*

He needs to have a basic descriptive knowledge of his faith—its sacred writings, its doctrines, its moral teachings, its organization, its rites, its history, its exemplary stories. We often find this information codified in mnemonic formulae—Four Holy Truths, the Eightfold Path, the Five Pillars, the Ten Commandments—so that it can be ensured that all the laity have what is considered to be the necessary minimum of descriptive knowledge.

2 *Anamnesis and historical knowledge*

The believer is a member of an historical community, and his historical knowledge is not just the sort of knowledge we might have of the early history of Egypt or China. Nor is it just a matter of 'the past' being for him 'our past'. The community does not merely treasure its memories: it continually recalls its past and re-enacts

[2] You may say that at just this point in the argument I am performing a piece of sleight of hand, by objectifying the transcendent. I hope the whole argument will disarm this accusation, by making it clear that I have no interest in performing such a trick: for objectivity is itself one of the ideas that is in the end to be transcended.

the great events from which it sprang. The events thus take on
the status of *myths*. Through its act of recall (anamnesis) the
religious body transcends time, uniting itself with its source. The
Passover Haggadah, the Eucharist, the pilgrimage to Mecca, or
the recollection of the Buddha's night of enlightenment—it is here
that religion uses history in its own special way, to transcend time
and gain eternity. The believer's historical knowledge is analogous
to what Proust knew when he tasted the madeleine biscuit dunked
in tea, and regained past time. Suppose that Proust's first and
second tastings had been understood by him as religious experiences;
then the second, with its anamnesis of the first, would have shown
him how the Eternal transcends time.

3 *Practical skills*

Knowing-how-to is an important kind of knowing, and it figures
largely in religion. One has to learn how to pray, and how to partici-
pate in rituals. These skills, again, are systematically taught in
religious communities. But some skills are still more delicate and
hard to teach. They are acquired as one goes along, *ambulando*,
as an infant learns to speak. The skills I mean are indeed a
special sort of linguistic skills—they are the ability to handle
religious concepts correctly, the ability to apply teachings imaginatively in life-situations, the ability to use and not abuse religious
symbols.

For example, everyone has to cope in his life with moral evil
and suffering; and every religion offers believers certain resources
to help them do so. But one needs a good deal of skill to be able
to pick out and utilize these resources (whether theoretical or practical) correctly. Progress in the religious life largely consists in the
refinement of such skills.

Again, a religion offers a body of symbolism by which it represents
the goal of the religious life and our relation to it. It is not easy
to learn how best to use these symbols, especially since it often
happens that they suggest different things. For example, one often
finds a conflict between imagery of gradual progress in the religious
life (like climbing a mountain, or going on a pilgrimage) and
imagery of sudden change (like the passage from darkness to light,
or from death to rebirth). There was a vivid example of this in
a famous disagreement in Buddhism which came to a head at
Lhasa in about 800 C.E. The Indians held that it takes aeons to
reach Enlightenment, whereas the South Chinese Zen masters taught

that it could be achieved in an instant. There was a similar controversy over justification at the time of the Reformation in Europe. The fact is that in any great religious tradition one will find both sorts of imagery side by side. The skill lies in knowing which one to invoke on some specific occasion, and how to use it.

Something like this problem arises in the case of proverbs. Every culture has a stock of proverbial wisdom, expressed in short apophthegms. At first glance some of these sayings appear inconsistent with others. 'Look before you leap' seems to say the opposite of 'He who hesitates is lost'. The skill lies in knowing which one is relevant and how it is relevant, on some particular occasion.

4 *Moral knowledge*

Like the word 'philosophy', the word 'moral' has suffered a severe contraction of meaning in modern times. At least until the eighteenth century the moral realm embraced all the humanities, and moral subjects included everything pertaining to the human heart, human thought, and human conduct; from ethics to economics, from psychology to history, from the theory of knowledge to political theory. The moral knowledge which religion demands is perhaps closest to what would now be termed introspective psychology and ethics. Religion requires and enables a growing self-knowledge, and through that an understanding of the human heart, of human motivation, and of man as a moral being. By acquiring self-knowledge one gains practice in the intellectual leap to the transcendent; and increased understanding of oneself leads to an increase of moral freedom in the sense of capacity.

Religious self-knowledge is interestingly different in its methods and results from modern scientific psychology. Since modern psychology largely adopts the professed 'amoralism of method' which has been typical of modern natural science it results in a purely descriptive knowledge of human behaviour, from which in strict logic no moral inferences can be drawn. The result is that the sciences of man are in danger of producing a cultural condition of moral impotence. Since, in practice, they are often allied with such practical arts as medicine and social administration, we may hear a good deal of scientific moralizing: but such moralizing is unconscious, and has no acknowledged foundation.

Religious self-knowledge, on the other hand, has an explicit moral interest from the first, and has therefore a chance of providing a more useful body of moral knowledge. It sees human nature in teleological terms, as oriented towards the supreme goal of the moral life.

5 *Philosophy of life and the lessons of experience*

Every great religion has a characteristic 'ethos', a word which no doubt originally referred to customs and rituals, but which I use in the modern sense to mean its general outlook on life. It is connected with the basic doctrinal affirmations, and expresses itself in characteristic patterns of feeling and behaviour. One might cite as examples the traditional Jewish response to suffering, or the Jewish feeling about the family.

As one enters a religion and assimilates its ethos, its general outlook on life, one may gradually grow in 'wisdom'. The loss of the idea of wisdom is one of the saddest losses of modern culture, because it has largely emptied the second half of life of value and importance. So complete has been the loss that it is now difficult even to state what is meant by 'wisdom', and what kind of knowledge it is. The nearest surviving kinsman of it is the idea of a vast and long experience. But the idea of a person of great experience is the idea of someone ponderous and cautious, whereas wisdom was light, subtle and devastating. The best Eastern example is perhaps the sayings of Zen masters; the best Western examples are the dicta of the rabbis of the Hasidic revival, and the Catholic tradition of 'spiritual letters'. For others the Journals and Discourses of Kierkegaard are the best source of such material, once they have learnt to live with and allow for his strange personality.

Whence does wisdom get its levity? Precisely from the idea of the transcendent. For the wise man is the man who is so steeped in a religious programme, and loves it with such inwardness, that he transcends it spiritually, and both affirms it and mocks it. He knows both that the programme is the best that he or anyone else is capable of, and that it is nevertheless comically disproportionate. Indeed, he himself is comically incongruous with the transcendent.

6 *Personal knowledge*

The paradoxes of knowledge and ignorance, which lie at the centre of religion, bedevil discussion of the element in it of knowledge by acquaintance. If the transcendent is not directly knowable, how can personal communion with the divine be the heart of the religious life?

That the transcendent is not directly knowable is a common-place of post-Kantian philosophy, and is declared in different ways both in Western theism and in Buddhism. In early Buddhism the spirituality was so extraordinarily austere and exalted that both the gods and the self were in effect set aside as irrelevant to the spiritual life.

But how then can there be personal communion with an Other which is unknowable? Theistic faith projects upon the void a body of symbolism, it fantasizes a personal deity to whose will it becomes subject. But there is of course no way in which the symbol can be compared with the thing symbolized so as to assess its adequacy as a pictorial representation. However sympathetic we may be to the forces and motives which compel the believer to project his fantasy of a personal God, his communion with such a deity is in the end, surely, nothing *but* a fantasy. It cannot be described as a mode of knowledge.

The answer to this widely felt unease is this: the various elements in religious knowledge which have so far been described, put together, give the total programme through which the religious person addresses life. They are the attitudes, beliefs, and policies by which he proposes to orient his life and thought. He proposes to live (if he is a theist) as under the eye and care of a loving, holy, and powerful God. The religious knowledge which he has acquired gives a rich patterning or structure to his experience. It is confirmed in experience so far as in the actual living of the religious life it is found satisfying and productive of good results, morally, intellectually, and imaginatively. The sense in which one religious system is truer than another is not so very different from the sense in which Newton's cosmography is truer than Ptolemy's. The way Newton saves the appearances is more efficient, economical, intel-lectually fertile, and beautiful than the way Ptolemy does; and, not only that, it copes with certain situations of strain and difficulty better than Ptolemy.

That we do thus pattern our experience, and must do so, to make the world intelligible, should not at this stage need further explanation, but I will add another example. We impose a pattern upon time of days, weeks, months, and years. The origins of the seven-day week are lost in prehistory, but it is perhaps related to the seven visible planets (including the sun and the moon). Apart from the decimal week proposed at the time of the French Revolu-tion, there have been few serious attempts to change it. We perceive time in terms of the seven-day week, and abandoning it would be an enormous cultural change. One such change has taken place. Longer periods of time were once calculated in terms of generations of twenty, twenty-five, or forty years. Gradually people came instead to think in terms of a procession of centuries, and so of a world-wide time-scale in terms of which it could be clearly understood that the third regnal year of Sennacherib had been the same year as the twelfth regnal year of Hezekiah. Neither the week nor the century are units of time directly related to celestial periods in the way that the day, the month, and the year are. The week and the century are cultural creations by which we structure our working lives and our sense of history respectively.

The week, then, is a bit of our programming, something we apply to experience. It once had, and for some still has, religious authority.[3] It was God's will that human life should be so patterned. And it is arguable, though alternatives have not been very extensively tested, that the week has been vindicated in practice as giving a ratio of work-periods to rest-periods that is about right. Shift-workers who maintain continuous industrial processes and have to work in nine-, ten- or twelve-day cycles do not seem very happy about it; and there are other circumstances, at sea, in war, and so on, where the ordinary seven-day cycle has to be abandoned with considerable physiological discomfort. So here is a case, perhaps, where practice has in general vindicated a bit of seemingly arbitrary patterning of experience.

Belief in God, then, can be explained in three stages. First, there is the abstract idea of the transcendent. Any adequate account of human intelligence must make reference to it, and the absence of such a reference is what makes people rightly indignant with reductive and manipulative psychologies such as that of B. F. Skinner. The idea of the transcendent is presupposed in the mind's creative leap to a new standpoint, whether in knowledge, morality, religion, or humour.

In the second place there is the content given to the idea of God (conceived, obscurely, as the objective transcendent) in religious belief. Fascinated with the transcendent, with the fact that it can

---

[3] Cities began because star-gazing priests drew from the heavens the time-patterns by which terrestrial life could be ordered. They gave the farmer the calendar he needed, to know when to sow his various crops. Thus the priests in their sanctuaries acquired the authority which drew people on pilgrimage to the holy places, and made them centres for worship, trade, and government.

exist as spirit, the mind tries to conceive pure spirit. It makes no progress. The best it can do is to relate itself practically to the transcendent. So religious belief programmes the mind to give a religious structure to its experienced world. This programming is the concrete content of the idea of God. It contains various elements—myth, doctrine, moral orientation, ritual, and other institutions.

Thirdly, the programme itself evolved over a long period and through various men's experience of life. The believer appropriates it as he gradually learns the religious life. He enters into a tradition, a fellowship of saints. The mental programme applied to the world discloses the meaning of the world. The world delivers up theistic sense, is found to lend itself more happily and completely to this interpretation than any other. What was a projection increasingly becomes a perception. One may when a non-swimmer looks dubiously at charts showing how to swim, and feel very uncomfortable when practising the strokes lying on one's belly along a bench, but when the lesson finally 'clicks' and one can swim, why, it is the simplest thing in the world.

KNOWING AND UNKNOWING

I am becoming Hegelian, for I am talking of the transcendent in something like the way Hegel talks of 'Geist' in *The Phenomenology of Spirit*; but, undeterred by this thought, we can now elaborate our idea of the transcendent as follows:

1. At the first stage the transcendent is our bare capacity for conceptual revolution. It is the gymnastic trick, the most powerful capacity of the human mind, by which in creative thought and in humour we can think the relation of our own thought to its object. When for some reason we are 'blocked' and cannot do this, tragedy arises, as a state of baffled incomprehension, which we obscurely know ought not to exist. We have introduced the transcendent in this sense in our prison metaphor, and in talking of the relation of our mental programmes to the world-meanings they yield as they are applied to experience. We invoked the notion of the transcendent in order to overcome the problem of relativism at this point.

2. Thinking of the transcendent, we may consider it *objectively*, as the absolute perspective from which human world-views can be compared, and which provides the Archimedean point by which

we can make the transition from one of them to another. The transcendent is what I grasp so as to swing from the complex (M^1W^1) to the complex (M^2W^2). But we can also consider the transcendent *subjectively*, as a human capacity—creative imagination or spirituality. That strain in European romanticism which says that man is a god who by his thought and action makes the world a finished creation begins from this point. Again, if in religion one begins from the transcendent subjectively understood, and seeks to focus the idea and refine it, the religious outcome is Buddhism.

There seems to be a crux at this point: shall the transcendent be thought objectively or subjectively? For reasons which will appear in due course I propose to follow the former way—and then negate it. This yields, I hope to show, a more powerful construction: and in some measure dissolves the distinction between the subjective and the objective transcendent into a question of the order of the exposition.

3. Theistic religion, then, thinks the transcendent objectively. It develops, through a great communal effort, a mental programming which projects human and this-worldly features upon the unknowable face of the transcendent. It generates a communal programme, shared and lived by believers, by which life in this world is so structured as to mediate personal communion with the transcendent. This communal programme is its entire theology and world-view —including myth, doctrine, morals, rituals, symbols, and visible institutions. Appropriating and living this programme, I structure my life in the world so as to experience it as a life lived in communion with a holy God. I claim authority and truth for my religion in so far as I find the complex whole (M^RW^R) intellectually, morally and aesthetically satisfying and fruitful. By its fruits I know that this is the right total attitude to life.

4. But the movement does not stop there. Were it ever to do so, religion would die. For the same restless aspiration after the transcendent which brought me thus far cannot but force me to take the next step, and relativize (M^RW^R) in turn. I become an iconoclast, I realize the primacy of the negative way, when I find that I am obliged to recognize the limitations of even the noblest religious system that can be devised. (M^RW^R) is, and must be, negated by yet another transcending leap of thought. But this further leap is a leap into the dark, into unknowing, because there cannot be any further whole (M^XW^X) after every possible interpretative framework has been found wanting—and it *must* be so found wanting by the

very nature of spirit. If all knowledge is relative to some conceptual scheme, to leave the last such scheme behind is to pass beyond the knowable. I negate my objectification of the transcendent—without knowing what the outcome is.

In this sense, then, Anselm's Ontological proof is valid, because it demonstrates that that which is at and beyond the limits of thought is necessarily the *terminus ad quem* of all philosophical and religious speculation. A high transcendent monotheism, in which the negative way, the way of unknowing, comes first, must be the final thought in matters of religion. This point was reached perhaps in Israel first, or perhaps in other places too at the same time, about twenty-five to thirty centuries ago, and it leaves nothing further to be said. The thought of the unsurpassable cannot be surpassed.

Now in so far as a religion has grasped and held fast to this insight, it will be found to teach not only the value of its own religious system (M^RW^R), but also, in its spiritual and iconoclastic mood, the relativity of that very system. The Upaniṣads teach this, and so do the Hebrew prophets, and so they have final authority, and teach the final truth.[4] Religion's last insight is its greatest: you can have knowledge in religion only in so far as you recognize that the last word is with unknowing.

5. Now comes something preposterous, a further step after what we have just established to be necessarily the last step. When we reach stage 4, and think about where we are, we realize that the spiritual life has brought us to a point at which we cannot state the difference between our position and agnosticism or scepticism, except by describing the moves which brought us to this point. We cannot kick away the ladder we have climbed, or we shall fall. And in institutional terms, it would be odd if a great religious community were found to consist of a mass of ordinary believers who affirm the images (at stage 3) gathered about a nucleus of proficients whose religion is refined to the point of emptiness and silence.

What happens is rather that religion lives in an enantiodromia (to use C. G. Jung's term), a constant flux and reflux between stages 3 and 4. This spiritual dance is the central source of intellectual and artistic creativity in any culture. When it is lost, as it is in

---

[4] 'God being hidden, any religion that does not declare him to be hidden is not true': Pascal's *Pensées*, 598 (Chevalier numbering).

danger of being lost today, the sources of life are cut.[5]

So in Christianity the faith is centred mythically upon the history of Jesus, a man who lived within the contemporary religious system and at the same time transcended it in his ability to criticize it and see clearly what was wrong with it. If Socrates' philosophical spirituality makes him the perfect Greek, Jesus is the most Jewish of Jews in his ability to mock ironically the very religious system to which he is so utterly dedicated, even to the extent of caricaturing God as an indolent judge or an absentee landlord. Could the Buddha have made a joke of Enlightenment?[6]

It is this fiery dance between the affirmation of images and their negation, between rapturous piety and the cry of dereliction, which is the heart of religion. For Jesus it ended with the cross, with death and loss, and the proclamation of the resurrection, not in or to this life and this world, but only beyond the grave. The dance between the poles issues in wisdom and gives to wisdom its lightness, detachment, and awesome sense of spiritual mastery.

We can now see in the right perspective the religious language of loss and gain, and its emphasis on renunciation. The best statement is that of St John of the Cross, in the poem prefixed to, and commented on in the course of, his book *The Ascent of Mount Carmel*. I quote from a prose paraphrase by Professor E. M. Wilson:

In order to have pleasure in all, seek not to have pleasure in anything.
In order to obtain all, seek not to obtain anything.
In order to be all, seek not to be anything.
In order to know all, seek not to know anything.

In order to taste what you taste not, you must go by the way of not tasting.
In order to reach what you know not, you must go by the way of not knowing.

[5] Kierkegaard says (*Journals*, XI'A 94) that 'the enormous development of the natural sciences in our time shows that humanity despairs of becoming spirit'. I would rather say that in the excitement of being involved in that development we may forget that it's only because we *are* spirit that it is possible. And if for long we forget that we are spirit then its correlate, the relativity of our knowledge, may take us unawares and terrify us. If we always remember that we are spirit we will never be surprised by it and indeed it will exhilarate and inspire us.

[6] Humour does enter Buddhism later, for example in the figure of Maitreya.

In order to obtain what you do not obtain, you must go by the way of not obtaining.

In order to be what you are not, you must go by the way of not being.

When you heed anything, you cease to leap to obtain all.

For in order to come wholly to all, you must deny yourself wholly to all.

And when you come wholly to possess, you must possess it without seeking anything.

For if you wish to have something in all, you have not your pleasure purely in God.

In this nakedness the spiritual soul finds her quiet and rest, for as she covets nothing, nothing urges her upwards, and nothing presses her downwards, because she is lying in the centre of her humility; for when she desires anything, in that thing she wearies herself.

In his spiritual Canticles St John repeatedly describes the ascent of the mind to God. The last stage in which he 'seizes his prey' is a condition in which all knowledge is transcended (*Toda sciencia transcendiendo*) and the self seems entirely burned away (*Todo me voy consumiendo*):

> The more I rose into the height
> More dazzled, blind and lost I spun.
> The greatest conquest ever won
> I won in blindness, like the night.
> Because love urged me on my way
> I gave that mad, blind, reckless leap
> That scared me up so high and steep
> That in the end I seized my prey.
> (trans. Roy Campbell)

The metaphor of leaping which St John uses here (*oscuro salto*), and which I have invoked more than once, has often suggested to people that the 'leap of faith' is irrational. This is not so. It can often happen that one attacks a problem head-on, and battles against it, and finds that the more one struggles the less progress one makes. One beats one's head against the wall until one is quite stupid. But then one may in a fit of inspiration, or even from mere fatigue, relax one's energies, draw back, recollect oneself, step sideways, look again at the problem and the way one was trying to tackle it, and suddenly see that the difficulties were largely of one's own making. A different approach, and the whole shape of the problem changes and it becomes manageable. There is nothing irrational about this manoeuvre.

The sudden relaxation or surrender of the will by which the trick is done can often be observed just before a man dies, and it may have suggested to Tolstoy the deathbed repentance described in *The Death of Ivan Ilyich*: the point being that there is an affinity between the act by which one surrenders the will to live and is able to die and the acts of faith by which one repents and is saved. A deathbed repentance coalesces the two, to make an artistically beautiful whole. What is more, it provides an artistically apt setting for treating the problem of evil. Existentialist interpreters of the story usually regard Ilyich's struggle as the struggle of one who, though he realizes that people in general die, cannot accept that he, Ivan Ilyich, must die. But Tolstoy's text plainly shows Ilyich wrestling with the problem of evil, taking up a self-righteous posture, accusing God and saying, 'Why is this happening to me?' To one who takes up such a stance, death is an invincible enemy; and the problem of evil, so formulated, intractable. Ilyich's struggles and sufferings are Promethean. At last he is exhausted by the sheer violence of his suffering, and the shift of perspective is brought about: he looks at the problem of evil in a different way, and repents. Death vanishes, light takes its place, his body relaxes— and he dies.

A similar shift must take place if one is to enter upon the right attitude to time. People have, especially in our highly secularized culture, a disordered apprehension of time. It appears demonic and terrifying. In obsessional neurosis the past has become a prison that traps the spirit; in anxiety it is the future which causes alarm. For others the experience of moral freedom in the present moment is dreadful, for it imposes an intolerable burden of responsibility. The past thrusts upon us a remorse for the unalterable, and habits that cannot be shaken off; the uncertainties of the present and future sap the will. The past weakens us because we know too much of it, the present and future because we know too little. The secularized notion of time current in our culture creates a situation of bondage to time. The only escape from it is by precisely the *metanoia*, the mental shift, which I have been describing, and by which one becomes spirit and enters upon eternal life.

There is nothing irrational in all this, unless (as can too easily happen) our concept of rationality has become internal to a *Weltanschauung*, a particular (M^XW^X) way of thinking. If that be allowed to happen, then of course it is by definition irrational to look for a way of escape from one's intellectual bondage. The concept of rationality has been defined in such a way as to create that bondage and maintain it. Unfortunately, in a great deal of modern philosophy Kant's criticism of dogmatic metaphysics has been used to justify a kind of positivism which falls, or rather deliberately walks, into just that trap. The simplest reply to it is that if it were true, originality in morals, in art, in religion, and in speculation would be impossible. But they are possible, because they do occur; and so it is untrue.

But what of knowledge? I have conceded that all our knowledge is relative to particular conceptual schemes, to particular (M^XW^X) systems. I have urged at length that that statement itself implies the possibility of transcending the relativities of our various conceptual schemes. But where they are transcended we pass beyond the knowable. Hence in religious thought the supreme object of the religious quest is declared to be unknowable. It is dimly apprehended, it is said, in unknowing, or in a knowledge beyond knowledge, or in a state which transcends knowledge. The morality play *Everyman* makes the point clear. As Everyman approaches the grave all his friends desert him, except Knowledge (that is, the knowledge of God) and Good Deeds. Good Deeds, in accordance with mediaeval theology, will accompany him through death. The case with Knowledge is slightly different:

EVERYMAN	Knowledge, wyll ye forsake me also?
KNOWLEDGE	Ye, Eueryman, whan ye to Deth shall go;
	But not yet, for no maner of daunger.
EVERYMAN	Gramercy, Knowledge, with all my herte
KNOWLEDGE	Nay, yet I wyll not from hens departe
	Tyll I see where ye shall be-come.

(858-63)

Though Knowledge cannot go with Everyman through death, he does remain standing by the graveside as he descends. Then Knowledge says that he thinks that he can faintly hear the singing beyond.

So religious knowledge looks at last beyond itself. At its simplest it is factual knowledge about the teachings, the myths, the history, and the rites of a religion. As we appropriate these and live by them we enter into a religious world-view, (M^RW^R). In this religious world-view we experience the meaning of life as, for example, a dialogue with a holy God. We have moved a step further in religious knowledge. The next step is to realize that this knowledge is relative to (M^RW^R), which we must at last leave behind. The third level of religious knowledge, beyond the conceptual scheme of practical religion, is unspeakable and is only enjoyed in and by death, or in a condition so like death as to be beyond language. To lay hold on it, so far as possible in this life, one must be willing to enter this death-like state. Though it is the climax of the religious life, it does not actually verify (M^RW^R) as some have suggested.[7] It quite plainly cannot do that, because it is of a different order altogether.

---

[7] So that I disagree with Professor John Hick's notion of 'eschatological verification'.

7

The Supreme Value of
the Transcendent

We have been seeking to explain what religious knowledge is, and
why it should be sought, in terms that stand a chance of being
applicable to both theistic and non-theistic religions. My presump-
tion has been that Buddhism, in particular, has such manifest intellectual weight that it is worth trying to keep within hailing distance
of it: and I believe that, surprising though it seems, there are
many principles of religious knowledge common to theistic and
non-theistic faiths. Our account of the nature of religious knowledge has suggested how it is possible for seemingly very acute
doctrinal differences between belief-systems to arise.

The difference between theistic and non-theistic religion does
become sharper, though, now that we turn to ethics. Our description
of religious knowledge so far has suggested, indirectly, some sort
of characterization of its ultimate object—or rather, has suggested
the shape of its indescribability. We have now to ask, what gives
the object of religious concern its supreme moral authority and
worth? The question needs to be asked because hitherto we have
discussed the transcendent and our relation to it mainly in speculative rather than in practical terms. This has caused a certain imbalance, which must now be corrected.

Our earlier argument may suggest that we make use at this point
of a distinction made by H. L. Mansel in the seventh of his
Bampton lectures,[1] between absolute and relative morality. For
Mansel, absolute morality is coeternal with, and identical with, the
nature of God himself; and for Mansel himself, of course, it is
unknowable. Human moralities, including even the revealed will
of God, are adaptations or accommodations of this absolute
morality to the contingent circumstances of human life. The Ten
Commandments, for example, are relative to an order of things
in which one moral agent can kill another, and in which there
are such institutions as marriage and private property. Mansel

[1] *The Limits of Religious Thought Examined* (London, 1858).

was not an ethical relativist in the modern sense; he was arguing that, since absolute morality is unknowable, we should be content to accept on the authority of revelation a morality for this life which, we are assured, is in the wisdom of God the best adaptation of it to our situation. Morality, as we can know it, must be relative to ourselves, as we are. Kant, according to Mansel, had held that there are knowable necessary truths in morals, by means of which we can criticize revelation: and so Mansel objected to Kant's critique of revelation by denying the premiss upon which it was carried out.

For Mansel, there was one relative morality which, though relative, was supremely authoritative: but, taking his distinction out of his own context, and relating it to our own consciousness of moral change and moral relativity, we might say that the notion of a transcendent or absolute morality is necessary to overcome the puzzles caused by the evident variety of human value-systems and moral codes.

In fact, however, I do not want to say this. Ever since men of different cultures first coexisted in the same State, sceptical men have noticed differences of moral belief: Herodotus[2] tells a tale of Darius making fun of such differences. But so far as I can see the moral disagreements here are—or have not been shown *not* to be —merely the consequence of differences of world-view; differences, that is, in the way the facts appear in relation to different interpretative frameworks. As such, ethical relativism is simply an aspect of the general problem we have been discussing.

The reason for this is that even the strongest 'prescriptivist', who most sharply disjoins the realm of nature and indicative statements from the realm of morals and imperative statements, must allow that indicative premisses enter into many valid moral arguments; and that if they are changed the imperative conclusions of those arguments will be different. Consider such 'practical syllogisms' as the following:

1   All doors ought to be shut (imperative).
2   This door is open (indicative).
3   Therefore this door ought to be shut (imperative).
and
1   Stealing is wrong (imperative).
2   A is an act of stealing (is of such-and-such a character and falls under such-and-such a definition—indicative).

[2] Book III, 37f.

3   Therefore A is wrong (imperative).

It is therefore clearly possible for cultural differences, and for the way the facts are seen differently under different cultural perspectives, to generate substantial moral disagreements, especially at the level of casuistry. So far as I know, those who draw attention to 'ethical relativity' have not demonstrated anything more than this: and as such it is a problem we have already considered.

How else might ethics be thought of as demanding the notion of the transcendent? One suggestion is that in situations of moral perplexity we need to be fortified by the idea that omniscience knows what is right, even if we do not. We need to make heuristic use, at least of the idea of an absolute moral knowledge: more strongly, in moral perplexity we might pray for guidance in the confidence that God knows, and will tell us, what is the right thing to do.

Unfortunately conflicts of duties are real: there are situations in which to discharge one duty is to neglect another, and it is superstitious to suppose that there *must* be a course of action by which evil can be entirely avoided. It would be clearly wrong to invoke the transcendent, or to pray, under this misapprehension, instead of calculating which is the least evil of the available courses of action.

There is a third possibility, that we must invoke the transcendent in order to describe and explain the overriding or peremptory character of the claim of what we know to be our duty. Moral obligation is itself of transcendent and unconditional sacredness. Kant himself may not have thought so,[3] but it is conceivable that the supreme authority of the moral law may be quite independent of whatever may be the case about the universe, however blind or hostile to morality it may be. If so, moral obligation might come to be seen as our *only* link with the transcendent: the notion of the transcendent can have no other content than the knowledge that in morality and there alone do we transcend the world-process which enmeshes us. If this be true, then our present inquiry after religious knowledge must terminate with the affirmation that it consists of nothing else but our knowledge that we are subject to moral obligation. However, our argument as a whole is against this opinion.

[3] Keith Ward, *The Development of Kant's View of Ethics* (Oxford, 1972), pp. 84ff.

So it may be suggested that the idea of the transcendent is required in morals precisely to reassure us in the fact of the bleak possibility we have just been considering. We need the idea of the transcendent to guarantee that what ought to be will in the end coincide with what is, both in ourselves and in the world about us. The object of religious aspiration is deemed to be of supreme intrinsic value, and its pursuit the chief purpose of life, because it is a condition of the possibility of actually living the moral life that it shall actually achieve something; that we will in the end realize the moral ideal. The beliefs in God and immortality assure us that moral striving is in the end fruitful, and is not defeated by the intractability of human nature, the amorality of physical nature, and our own deaths. Why struggle to no avail? In the realm of nature human life does peter out; so the moral goal must be sought beyond that realm. But in thought we can and do transcend the realm of nature. Thus we conceive the transcendent as identical with the moral goal, as that in which both the contemplative and active sides of human life find their final fulfilment.

But this line of thought is open to obvious objections. Obligation may be absolute, but it does not obviously and immediately follow that we are obliged to seek and must be capable of attaining absolute perfection. I ought to do the examination paper as well as I can, but it does not follow that I am under an obligation to obtain 100 per cent marks, still less that I will be allowed an infinite time in order to do so. How do we know that a being can be both human and morally perfect? Perhaps it can only be one, and not the other. The obligation to do all that is in one's power will still stand even if one cannot do everything: there is no *contradiction* in saying, 'Do all you can; I know you can't do everything.' In the same way, the civil law ought to be ordered by moral principles, but a man may be a zealous social reformer even though he fully recognizes that there can never be, in this wicked world, a perfect human society. Such a man may well do more good than the man with a blueprint for Utopia. Kant's famous arguments are clearly reminiscent of Aquinas's Fourth Way, the argument that for us to be able to grade things as being more or less P we must suppose that there is something which is absolutely P, and more than that, there must actually *be* something which is absolutely P. And there seems no way of defending this argument. Even the more modest psychological claim that the idea of moral perfection is needed to motivate our moral striving is open to criticism. Greyhounds are induced to run round a dog-track by a mechanical rabbit which is kept just out of their reach; but a mechanical rabbit which moved immeasurably faster than they would merely discourage the hapless dogs. I may be more effectively encouraged by someone only a little better than myself than by someone immeasurably better than myself.

So, after all these preliminaries, we have still not discovered the point at which the transcendent bears upon the moral life, and comes to be identified with the goal of moral endeavour. The answer is to be found in a direction in which Kant did not think to look. None of his contemporaries believed more devoutly than he that a man could and must perfect himself by his own efforts. Kant thought that we could reason out what the moral virtues are, and adopt maxims of conduct whereby we progressively actualize these virtues in ourselves. We know *a priori* that the highest good is attainable by our own efforts, and we must therefore presume that the conditions of its attainability (the postulates of practical reason) are fulfilled.

We have just been criticizing this very argument, at the point where it moves from *We are subject to moral obligation* to *We are obliged to attain, and it is therefore in our power to attain, the Highest Good*. And how very odd, in terms of the history of human culture, is this conviction that we know what the Highest Good is, that we know we are obliged to attain it, and that we can capture it by our own moral striving! Such a confidence in our capacity to attain our own final good by our own efforts is very uncommon. It is much more usual, in the literature of religion and wisdom, to find the sages stressing the vanity of human striving. The pagan on that account gave himself up to sceptical ease in a tranquil suspense of mind. The Indian, on a rather different tack, sought a state in which desire is extinguished and the mind inactive, a condition which allows the peace of Enlightenment to descend upon him. His ethic is not directed towards attaining Enlightenment by force, but is rather an ascetical ethic designed to produce the stillness which can allow Enlightenment to realize itself in him. Moral endeavour does not seize Enlightenment, but shrinks back to allow it to disclose itself. The Christian has gone through ethical striving and been brought by it to despair, the consciousness of sin, and the felt need of Grace: this sequence makes it possible for a new kind of moral life to be realized in him by Grace. The pagan, the Indian, and the Christian, here so hastily sketched, all disagree with Kant, denying that through moral striving we can directly seize the highest good for ourselves, and attain our own final happiness.

To make the claim that the highest good is attainable by our own strivings even moderately plausible it is necessary to pare down one's account of what virtues are desirable, and what ends of action should be adopted. So Kierkegaard remarked that Kant's way to virtue by self-legislating will was no more serious or painful than the blows which Sancho Panza inflicted on his own posteriors. For the virtues Kant commends are as follows: (i) one should preserve in oneself the teleology of one's animal nature, avoiding self-inflicted injuries such as suicide, masturbation, and gluttony; (ii) one should preserve oneself in one's moral nature, avoiding self-deception, greed, and servility; (iii) one should cultivate one's own natural and moral powers; (iv) one owes a duty of benevolence to other men—being beneficent, grateful, and sympathetic rather than envious, ungrateful, or malicious; and (v) one owes a duty of respect for the dignity of others as moral agents, avoiding arrogance, slander, and mockery. The entire system is centred upon the notion of a society of free moral agents, each of whom affirms his own dignity and respects that of others: the kind of life, perhaps, that the complacent burgesses painted by the Dutch masters fancied themselves to be leading.

One might make moral criticisms of this picture of the good life; and one might point out that by the time Kant came to write his book on *Religion Within the Limits of Reason Alone* he had himself come to wonder whether even this modest ideal was within the reach of men as they actually are. Yet even in this book Kant will still not allow Grace to enter constitutively into the moral life, lest it derogate from the supreme value of moral struggle. He allows it only the status of a regulative idea. And when he introduces the idea of conversion, it is still no gift from the transcendent: it is merely deduced from the *a priori* conviction that however great the actual wickedness of the human heart, reason must be capable of overcoming evil by its own power; so that conversion must be logically possible, however rare it is in fact.

If the conviction that we can achieve the *summum bonum* is declared to express an *a priori* and necessary truth, what argument can there be against it? Only one, that it is internally incoherent: that the very notion of moral goodness is such that it is absurd to suppose that it can be attained by Kantian methods. And that is what I do in fact hold: neither the pursuit nor the possession of moral goodness can be entirely conscious and deliberate. Solemn moralists often argue that happiness cannot be directly pursued, but arises only as a by-product in men whose minds are fixed on something else: but if this is true of happiness, it is still more true of moral goodness.

For moral goodness suddenly evaporates, it collapses into the merest childish boasting, when it becomes conscious of itself. Job's long, self-laudatory speech (Job 31), in which he defends his own virtue, only succeeds in making the speaker appear ridiculous. The uttering of it falsifies it: it might all have been true—if only he had not wanted to say it. Job's moral goodness might have been genuine if he had remained unconscious of it, in accordance with the witty precept of the Gospel, 'Let not your left hand know what your right hand is doing.' The point of the secrecy about moral action enjoined in the Gospel is not that the agent must hug his own virtue to himself, but (more searchingly) that it must remain secret even from himself. Indeed Jesus's irony leads him to tell a story in which a man who correctly judges himself to be a wrong-doer is more righteous than a man who correctly judges himself to be righteous (Luke 18.9-14).

Failure to see this point creates an oddly embarrassing moment in the *Buddhacarita*, the earliest life of the Buddha. The newly-Enlightened Buddha meets five mendicants in the Deer Park at Kashi. Knowing his past, they are at first inclined to laugh at him, and even though his manner subdues them, they persist in disrespectfully addressing him by his family name. He rebukes them with a gentle and compassionate lordliness—and the reader is embarrassed. True, in a Buddhist context one could not attribute to Shakyamuni any self-defensive reflexes: he has no self any more which he might have an interest in defending. But still the reader is embarrassed, for even in that metaphysical context the nature of morality is such that no one, not even the Buddha, should be so secure in the knowledge of his own unshakeable virtue that he can with unruffled calm rebuke people who fail to recognize it.[4]

The concept of humility does not so much designate a particular

---

[4] The reason for the mistake is this: because moral goodness is of eternal worth, people begin to imagine it as rock-like. But alas, as realized in actual men, it is of the utmost frailty, and can be lost in a moment. As in religious experience we apprehend the eternal, but only in an instant which cannot be grasped, so in morality we may be of eternal worth, but only for a moment.

virtue, as rather draw our attention to the way in which the entire pursuit and possession of moral goodness must be veiled in order to exist at all. Others can recognize it, but not the agent: nor can anyone speak to the agent about it. If you and I speak together, we can very sensibly agree that some third person is a good man, but not that you are, or that I am.

The principle still holds even in relation to Grace. A leading theme of John Wesley's preaching was that 'Christian perfection' was readily attainable. It could be had by anyone who underwent a second conversion and entered upon 'the Great Salvation'. God's will was that all Christians should attain to 'Scriptural Holiness', and he would realize it in those who truly desired it. Wesley insisted upon the simple truth of this message, yet he would not claim himself to have entered upon this state, even though he insisted that it was for all, and was easy to be had. When some of his associates took the next step and did claim perfection, moral disaster overtook them. Wesley's mistake was to promise deliverance from conscious sin, and the attainment of conscious perfection:[5] but the leap of reason promises deliverance from sin of which, before that *metanoia*, one is precisely *un*conscious; and it promises a goodness which will be unconscious; must be, to be truly what it is, the gift of the transcendent.

Kant was wrong, I say, because there is an internal inconsistency in the very ideas of deliberately pursuing or consciously possessing moral goodness. If we imagine an actual man saying, 'I am doing this in order to make myself a better man', or saying, 'I am a good man', we can see the absurdity. In the Gospels Jesus says, 'Why callest thou me good? There is none good save one', and, 'Who made me a judge or divider over you?' There is no inconsistency between Jesus's denial of his own moral perfection and his followers' attribution of it to him. There would rather be something odd about a man who said, 'I am a good man', and his friends' agreement, 'Yes, you are': for there cannot be a consciously virtuous man. To a spiritual man, a consciously virtuous man is patently ridiculous.

So morality, if it is to flourish, needs to be checked—we might almost say, by a sense of its own relativity. If the moral realm is an autonomous realm of thought and action, and if moral principles have unconditional authority in our lives, our obligations are un-

[5] See R. N. Flew, *The Idea of Perfection in Christian Theology* (Oxford, 1934), XIX.

limited. We must strive to become ever more and more high-principled, to assume ever greater responsibility, and to seek purity of heart with ever greater diligence—and there can be no standpoint from which we can check our own headlong rush through moralism to fanaticism and moral collapse. Hyperactive striving can only see itself as obliged conscientiously to repress any thought of its own absurdity, and take itself ever more seriously. There is no way of self-consciously eliminating self-righteousness.

So the transcendent enters into the moral realm as that unknowing and unknown through which and from which supreme moral goodness is alone attainable. Moral virtue must be received as a free gift, in humility, because I cannot create it in myself by my own efforts. It will only ever be mine in so far as I think of it as *not* being mine. I cannot consciously possess it as my own creation in myself. Kant's self-made virtue is morally ridiculous: he was led astray by his individualism. We are morally obliged, if we value moral goodness above all else, never to claim to have created it in ourselves, but to reserve it to the transcendent: and only in so far as we relate ourselves to the transcendent in the knowledge of our own absurdity can we hope to attain it.

Now at last we have come to the parting of the ways: for ethics decisively separates theistic from non-theistic religion. Once again, I have Buddhism mainly in mind. Now, in non-theistic religion ethics does not reveal the nature of the transcendent. We find instead a self-negating ethic whose function is to bring action to a halt, to extinguish all desire, liberate us from the empirical self, and produce perfect stillness of mind. The resulting blank is filled with the peace of Enlightenment. Clearly Enlightenment itself cannot be described in personal or moral terms, because the personal, the moral, everything that is of this world must be entirely voided before Enlightenment can appear. It is beyond good and evil. If it is called peace, that means only absence of movement; and if bliss, that is the state of one who has no desires.

According to my argument, however, to attain an active and non-ascetical moral goodness we are morally obliged to believe in Grace, to regard the transcendent as the source of those supremely precious moral virtues which are necessarily secret.[6] That is, those

---

[6] Contrast this account with that of W. G. MacLagen, *The Theological Frontier of Ethics* (London, 1961), chs. 4 and 5. He works in the main with the post-Kantian assumption that constitutive Grace is subversive of morality, but in his careful discussion now and again makes points that I would want to seize upon.

aspects of moral goodness which we cannot without absurdity think to create in ourselves by conscious and deliberate effort are to be regarded as bestowed by the transcendent. So the way the transcendent is related to our thought is paralleled by the way it expresses itself in the moral life.

The qualities I have particularly in mind are, of course, spontaneous, unselfconscious, and disinterested love, generosity, and sympathy: everything embraced by the word *dilectio*, delight. Theistic ethics is under a moral necessity to ascribe such moral qualities to the transcendent, and so (within its programme) to speak of him as personal and as the final good.

8

Conclusions

Now we can draw some threads together, consider the argument as a whole, and see what light it throws on the problems with which we began.

1 PLURALISM

We started with the fact that modern societies are pluralistic. People of a variety of religions, cultural backgrounds, moral and political opinions, and ideologies coexist. The *interpretative plasticity of the world* seems to make it possible for human groups to survive and flourish with very different world-views, especially if we consider a world-view as an *action-guiding belief-system*. It is not easy to see how we can talk of objectivity or of truth, when we are considering such a complete belief-system, because the system has its own internal criteria of meaning and truth. It is in an odd way *self-verifying* and so self-reinforcing and self-perpetuating.

2 SUBJECTIVISM

One possible compromise is to regard logic, mathematics and the sciences as rational and objective; and to regard matters of belief and ideology, matters like ethics, religion, politics, and so on, as matters in which truth is 'subjective' only. The traditional tough-minded sort of British empiricism has tried to make a distinction of this kind. An item of scientific knowledge can be verified by demonstrating that it corresponds to or is systematically connected with observable features of the objective external world. But to prove the objectivity of scientific knowledge in this way we need to have 'pure' experience of the objective world, prior to any ideological interpretation. There has to be some element of the sheerly given, about which there can be no doubt. The system of scientific knowledge can then be shown to be constructed in an orderly way out of this sheerly given. And it is this sheerly given, these 'facts' or pure data, which are turning out to be very elusive.

Now the older arguments for scepticism claimed that since our senses admittedly *sometimes* deceive us, then for all we know they may be deluding us *all* the time. To this it was replied that to state the premiss of that claim is to admit that we can broadly distinguish times when our senses are deluded from times when they are not. Provided most of our sense-experience is coherent, the fact that a little of it is plainly not so need not force us into scepticism.

Modern knowledge, however, is creating a much more difficult and fluid situation. It used to be suggested that *yellow* is a simple quality, and that 'I seem to see yellow' is the sort of basic, sheerly given observation report upon which the fabric of empirical knowledge could be reared. But alas, there is no yellow receptor in the retina; yellow can be made by mixing red and green light, or by flashing the right mixture of black and white, or even by mixing red and white. The candle flame is yellow by day and white by night. Colour vocabularies are socially relative, and colour experience seems to be different in different cultures, as even the Latin and Greek use of colour words reminds us. Colour discrimination is at least partly (not entirely) a matter of cultural programming. It is an achievement of the brain, and not just of the supposedly passive eye. So not even seeming-to-see-yellow can be regarded as being presented with the sheerly given, prior to any programmatic interpretation.

So the distinction between the sheerly given and the construction which we place upon it is becoming harder and harder to make with confidence. And this is being recognized all through the sciences, though most markedly in the sociology of knowledge. Consider, for example, the extraordinary difficulty of defining non-prejudicially the difference between common-sense beliefs and superstitions, discussed by Gustav Jahoda.[1]

3 RELATIVISM

Hence the pervasiveness of the problem of relativism. Many philosophers have been in various ways concerned with the problem, and we have mentioned Marx, Collingwood, and the later Wittgenstein as examples. But more influential, perhaps, have been developments within the sciences. What were once taken to be universal truths constitutive of the world are now more and more seen

[1] *The Psychology of Superstition* (Allen Lane, The Penguin Press, 1969).

in programmatic terms, that is, as 'models' or 'conventions' with a limited range of application, which we may on occasion find it appropriate to discard and replace with something else. Euclid's axioms, and the basic concepts of Newton's physics, are examples.

And in the sciences of man, the insistent emphasis on the *causes* of beliefs has inevitably led to our seeing people's opinions as relative to their psychological make-up or their social situation.

4 PROGRAMMES

We coined the term 'programme' as a general term for the apparatus by which we 'put a construction upon' our experience. A programme is a complex interpretative framework by using which we make the world intelligible, and give meaning to action within it.

5 THE LEAP OF REASON

Yet our very ability to grasp the problem of relativism suggests the possibility of transcending it. How otherwise is conceptual revolution possible? When we think the relation of our own thought to its object, of programme to knowledge gained through it, we transcend ourselves in a *leap of reason*. The chief examples I have given are creative originality in thought, moral regeneration, religious iconoclasm, and humour.

When for some reason the leap of reason is blocked, and we are trapped in a state of dissatisfied incomprehension which we obscurely know to be wrong, but cannot escape, *tragedy* arises. A successful performance of the leap of reason creates *comedy*, the highest art form.

6 SUBJECTIVE AND OBJECTIVE

Our ability thus to transcend ourselves in freedom is what marks us as spirit. Our highest rational faculty is identical with our *freedom*. The standpoint which the leap of reason attains I call the *transcendent*.

How shall we understand the transcendent? We may try to understand it subjectively, affirming our own autonomous spirituality. The result, in art, is *Romanticism*. Since we cannot think our own spirituality, in itself, except as a contentless, autonomous energy which creates and destroys all the various possible programmes impartially, the outcome of a purely subjective understanding of the transcendent is, it seems to me, anarchy and pessimism. The initial problems from which we began remain unsolved. Wearied, the spirit turns away from the world in an ascetical revolt, and rests in its own emptiness. So I would regard the philosophy of Schopenhauer as mediating between Romanticism and *Buddhism*, as the religious expression of the subjectively conceived transcendent.

Suppose then, that the transcendent be conceived objectively, with a view to grounding it in the possibility of objective knowledge and moral virtue? It supplies the spirit with its laws of thought and action.

7 ACTIVE RELIGION

Active theistic religion attempts this. It evolves an exceedingly complex programme for interpreting experience and guiding action, with elements in it of myth, doctrine, ethics and ritual. The apparatus of active religion is anthropomorphic and its chief interest is in the effective guidance of action. The resulting structure has great ethical strength. But comprehensive though it is, active religion is still a programme, and it would be spiritually yet another prison if it did not contain within itself an iconoclastic or autodestructive principle. And so it does. The true religion is the religion which declares itself untrue, which asserts the relativity of its own symbolism and says that God is infinitely greater than our highest ideas of him. In this way we can allow for a measure of pluralism: a variety of religious programmes, each relative, may witness in different ways to the one God who transcends them all.

Some religious believers will certainly charge me with 'syncretism' at this point. But I reply that there *is* this sort of diversity, not only between the great religions, but within each of them. Christianity, for example, is not one, but a family of programmes in itself.

8 CONTEMPLATIVE RELIGION

Having conceived the transcendent objectively, the spirit must next transcend the concept of objectivity. So by a fresh leap of reason the spirit transcends active religion, into emptiness and unknowing, a kind of anticipation of death. And in practice religious life is lived between the poles of the warm, moralistic anthropomorphism of active religion and the clear, cold emptiness of contemplation.

So it was not a waste of time to take the objective route. The objective way gives the spirit humility, intellectual and moral. The glimpse of an unknowable absolute before which the various relativities of life fall into place gives the spirit courage, and *impels* it to return and accept the world.

Hence the odd paradox, that it is non-theistic religion which turns ascetically away from the world, lacking the courage to accept relativity, evil and suffering: whereas it is theistic religion which, precisely because God can be known only through the programme and not as he is in himself, sends the spirit back to the programme, and to acceptance of the world, to acceptance of the relative and the finite.

9 THE OBJECTIVITY OF KNOWLEDGE

And what of the objectivity of knowledge, religious and secular? I have suggested that the programme of active theistic religion is true precisely in so far as it courageously affirms its own relativity. I begin to know just in so far as I know that I do not know.

The objectivity of science is similarly grounded. If we would vindicate it we should point, not to a solid body of knowledge achieved, but to its intellectual humility in being perpetually ready to accept correction: the true scientific spirit.

And here we return at last to our starting-point, our ambiguous feelings about pluralism, about the explosively rapid growth of knowledge in our time, and our fear of fragmentation and a pervasive relativism. Are we saying that the spread of relativism undermines belief in reason, and threatens social disintegration? No, for I have tried to reconcile reason and relativism, and suggest instead that the spread of relativism is a sign of spiritual vigour. The pluralism and relativism of modern culture, far from destroying rational belief in God, may lead us back to it. The philosophy of spirit outlined in this book is intended to show how that might be done.

What of the idea of God to which we have been led? I have argued that theistic religion is ethically superior to non-theistic religion, but I have also insisted upon a clear distinction between God-in-the-programme, the anthropomorphic deity of active religion, and God-in-himself, the unknown deity of contemplative aspiration. A distinction, but not a separation, between these two; for I have tried to bolt them together, from both sides.

For, in the first place, the programme of active religion contains within itself an assertion of its own relativity. It insists on being itself transcended: it will not allow itself to be regarded as a final set of answers or a codified system. It reminds us that God is pure spirit, we are flesh; that his thoughts are higher than our thoughts, and all our ideas about him comically inadequate; a regular topic of religious parables. So active religion, in order to live, must die: it must contain within itself the negation of itself. And in the second place, precisely because God-in-himself is unknowable, the spirit is forced back to the programme and to this-worldly action as the nearest to him that we can come. He cannot be known directly, so he must be loved in the neighbour.

T. R. Miles[2] described his version of theism as 'silence qualified by parables'. I have tried to insist both on the distinction between the level at which we must be silent, and the level at which we must speak in parables; and also on the ways in which the two levels are linked.

This interpretation of belief in God has considerable advantages. It suggests how one who is himself a theist might understand the diversity of religions in a positive way. Even within one religion, a certain amount of programmatic variegation, between individuals and between groups, might be no bad thing. But also, I want to claim that many of the standard intellectual difficulties of belief in God can be considerably eased from the starting-point I have proposed.

For example, how are prayers answered? My suggestion is that, if we adopt the programme of ethical monotheism and live it out, experience will be found to lend itself to this programme. The 'answer to prayer' is the way in which the life-experience of the theistic believer tends to ratify his own initial programme.

Now the superstitious person who believes in astrology may well make claims about the fulfilment of his horoscope very similar to the claims about prayer made by theists. Our idea of the 'interpretative plasticity of the world' accounts for this admitted fact.

Is there, then, any respect in which prayer to a personal God is better than consulting one's horoscope? Yes, there is: prayers to a personal God are integral parts of a world-view and pattern

[2] *Religion and the Scientific Outlook* (London, 1959).

of life which is ethically richer than, and so better than, astrological faith.

And finally, petitionary prayer must always be internally checked by a saving awareness of its own tendency to slip into eudaemonism and anthropomorphism. Our account of God makes it clear that active religion does and must contain such a corrective principle within itself. The final truth about God and man altogether transcends the level at which we solicit and expect to obtain favours from him. So Christian intercession ends, as Kierkegaard used to insist, with the Amen; let God's will, not ours, be done.

So in petitionary prayer there is a level at which we cannot but ask for things, and a level at which we know it is absurd to do so; and both are held together.

The second problem we shall consider is that of God's *providence*. Does God ordain everything that happens? Does he foreknow and foreordain the future? Classical philosophical theism answers yes, especially in Christianity and Islam. The doctrine has been that God is outside time and tense altogether. He is timeless: from his *nunc stans*, his eternal Now, he gazes upon the entire four-dimensional world-process as a single whole. He sees each individual human life as a four-dimensional frankfurter sausage, from birth to death in space and time, a rounded sempiternal whole. We should not think of him as foreordaining the future, because he does not *fore*ordain. He simply eternally ordains all things, for he is *actus purus*.

This account has been a good deal criticized lately, and with good reason.[3] A timeless, all-ordaining deity is difficult to think of as personal, or as acting. He cannot undergo any change, so it is hard to see how he can be spoken of as responding to human need, or as becoming Incarnate. It is hard to see how in his timeless simplicity he can involve himself in the manifold contingencies of history. His knowledge of time, and the way the world-process appears to him, become totally different from our perspective upon these things.

Morality is an obvious difficulty. How can a timeless God even tell which way time's arrow points? But he needs to know, if he is to understand our moral experience. Kurt Vonnegut, in his novel *Slaughterhouse Five*, imagines a war film of a bombing raid, run backwards. The dead and wounded are restored, buildings rise again from devastation, the overflying aircraft suck the poisonous

---

[3] See, for example, Nelson Pike, *God and Timelessness* (London, 1970); A. N. Prior, 'Formalities of Omniscience', *Philosophy* (1962); William Kneale, 'Time and Eternity in Theology', *Proc.Arist.Soc.* (1961).

bombs up from the city and carry them gently home. Back on the airfield they are unloaded, and in the munitions factory women, appropriately, perform the merciful task of dismantling them, and converting them to their original minerals. Miners then carefully put the minerals back into the good earth. How beautiful, that murder in reverse becomes miraculous healing! It clearly makes a great deal of difference to the morality of the process which way time's arrow points. But God is out of time altogether. He does not see time's arrow pointing in *either* direction. He sees the good parts and the evil parts of the process all bound together in one seamless whole. What to us seems to be caused by us, to him is evidently ordained eternally by himself. Those thinkers who have stressed the timelessness of God are inevitably led to an aesthetic view of evil: it contributes to the beauty of the whole as the dark passages contribute to the beauty of a painting. God cannot see evils as we see them, nor make moral judgements that are in any way like ours, nor know what historical contingency feels like to us; for all these things depend upon our relation to time—and God's is quite different. Such a metaphysical deity seems to be of little moral or religious use.

My alternative account runs as follows: within the programme we ascribe to God not absolute ordinance of the future, but merely all power to accomplish his purposes and make the good prevail. Now the difference between the past and the future is that the past is fully determinate, whereas the future is not. Some things about the future can be predicted, with varying degrees of confidence, but it is entailed by the very concept of the future that it cannot actually be *known* with certainty, even by God. All that active religion requires is the confidence that God has the power to pull the threads together and make his will prevail, whatever we do. Just so, out of the free actions of Jesus, Peter, Judas, Pilate, Caiaphas, and the rest God has wrought redemption, not by overruling their freedom, but by knitting together what they did into that whole which is the passion story.

In this way, within the programme, we can retain historical contingency and human freedom in combination with belief in God's historical providence. We think of God as quasi-historical, sharing our life-experience and interacting with us within it. Within this system of ideas we may speak of life 'after' death, as the final consummation to which the religious life points.

This way of thinking of God's relation to time and to individual lives is required by the programme of active religion. It is a way of thinking about God-in-relation-to-ourselves. It is not, of course, the final truth. The final truth we do not know. Our thinking and experience, and above all our moral action, are conditioned by time. We cannot think non-temporal personal life. There is no way of doing it, and metaphysicians should not pretend otherwise. It is vital to remember the limitations, indeed the relativity, of the programmatic picture of God and time, because if we took it too literally we might be led into absurd mistakes and moral difficulties. Nevertheless, we have to work with it.

The third, and last, idea we shall instance is that of *revelation*. The concept of a divine revelation is that of a communication from God to man, and therefore any account of revelation must satisfy two conditions. The revelation must be of God, and true to what he is; and it must be comprehensible to its addressee. From our perspective we can see at once what the central difficulty is: how can *both* requirements be met simultaneously? Anything that fulfils the one must surely fail to fulfil the other.

Thus it is, I think, clear that there cannot be a direct revelation of God himself, for it would not be comprehensible. God is not one who *happens* to be hidden and might in principle choose to come out of hiding and display himself: he *is* his hiddenness—it is a defining characteristic. There have been theologians who have used the phrase 'God reveals himself', but they did so in a fit of absent-mindedness. A theophany, in the 'literal' sense, is scarcely a frequent occurrence in the scriptures of the great religions. And even where one occurs, it can only be recognized through a programme. Again, it would seem that there cannot be supernatural communication of authoritative propositions about God, for not even by revelation can the limits of any possible discourse about God be overcome. Rather, revelation is only possible by a *kenosis*, an act of condescension by which God accommodates himself to our human faculties. Accordingly the most religiously beautiful account of revelation is that which pictures the divine as taking human form, and on the basis of that divine-in-human-form builds up the programme of active religious faith. All parts of the programme are traditionally traced back to him: the doctrine is the doctrine of Christ, the ethics is the law of Christ, the Church is his body, the sacraments belong to him, the ministry is descended from him, and the exemplary stories relate to him directly, or indirectly through what others have done by his inspiration.

But, as the programme derived from him is relative, so is he. He came to proclaim, not himself, but God. If *per impossibile* he were an absolute objectification of God, he would not have had to die. But there cannot be such an objectification; so he must die, and point beyond himself by doing so.

Thus if we say we believe in revelation, we acknowledge the authority of the programme, but we do not declare the programme *absolute*. The difficulties over the concept of revelation have arisen because people thought that the right way to proclaim its authoritativeness was to declare it absolute and irreformable. Jesus's utterance—mocking, elliptical, enigmatic—is as far removed from the style of the absolute legislator as it could be, but it has not prevented the mistake being made. Always he says, 'I am not telling you: what do you yourself think?', but still we insist that he is telling us, and try against all reason to make a system of him and his words.

The true revelation, then, is *indirect*. The programme is given, and grows out of Jesus, indeed. But always he insisted on (and at its best the programme continued his affirmation of) his own relativity, by his teasing humour.

PART TWO

Theological Essays

9

On Belief in God

It is not easy even to define our present task. It was traditionally called 'proving the existence of God', but there are formidable objections to such a description of it, as will soon appear. So let us instead begin with the undoubted fact that a very large number of people—Jews, Christians, Muslims, Sikhs, and many others—believe in God. It is clearly important to know whether that belief is capable of rational justification. I hope to show that it is.

But even this starting-point is not without problems. What is this thing called 'belief in God', which is supposed to be held in common by people of many different faiths? Is there anything definite in it which is generally abstractible from all the various religious contexts in which it occurs? Surely what counts as 'God', what counts as 'belief in God', and what counts as a 'justification' of that belief, are all of them specified in markedly different ways in different religious communities? What reasons can we have for claiming that everyone who believes in God believes in, at bottom, the same thing in the same way?

The difficulty is that an attempt to prove the existence of God philosophically must rest upon a definition of God which is trans-religious: it must proceed, that is, upon the assumption that there is some common metaphysical claim made by all the various theistic religions. But the Jew does not talk about God in general, but about the-God-who-has-revealed-himself-through-Moses; the Christian about the-God-who-is-the-Father-of-Jesus-Christ; and the Muslim about the-God-whose-prophet-is-Muhammad: and these are three different specifications of God. The philosopher who supposes that, underlying these three different specifications, there is an identical metaphysical doctrine capable of purely philosophical appraisal is surely assuming the truth of *syncretism*, which is itself a religious doctrine; and, moreover, one that each of those same three religions stoutly rejects.

When we read a book about Islam, or about Indian religions, we are made to learn several foreign words. It is a commonplace that the central religious concepts in any culture are the most untranslatable words of all. In each religion the basic religious terms, the meaning of belief, and the criteria of right belief are specified in a distinctive way which colours or influences the whole complex religious system. It is true by definition that no two religions can possibly return the same answer to the question of what authority must be consulted in what way in order to settle a dispute about right belief. So the problem is that the meaning and the method of justification of any particular religious belief are integrally bound up with the whole religious system to which it belongs: and the belief cannot be abstracted from that system without such severe distortion that the whole enterprise begins to seem futile.

So the philosopher of religion is in a dilemma. If he frames a trans-religious definition of God, and sets out to prove the existence of God as so defined, he will be accused of syncretism, and the result of his labours will be repudiated by the very believers whose central belief he purported to discuss. But if instead he adopts the specification of God proper to one particular religion, and seeks to remain true to that religion's way of speaking about God, he will be doing dogmatic theology, and not rational theology.

A similar situation can arise in political theory. A great number of states profess to be democratic republics. Suppose a well-intentioned philosopher sets out to show that a democratic republic is the best form of political organization: then he immediately meets the difficulty that the phrase 'a democratic republic' is very differently understood in different countries. How can there be a politically neutral general definition of it? But if he adopts one particular definition people will say, 'That is propaganda for one State, not a generally relevant piece of political theorizing'. And is not the word 'God' at least as context-dependent for its meaning as the phrase 'a democratic republic'?

There seems to be no end to the reasons why it is hard to prove the existence of God. Some people have argued that belief in God is quite intelligible, but happens to be false. Others have said that belief in God is intelligible, but cannot be justified. More recently it has been fashionable to claim that belief in God is meaningless, and so can be neither true nor false. But I am considering a more modern way of seeing the matter, according to which belief in God is above all a *religious* belief, which bears a specific meaning and is justified in relation to a particular religious community and its universe of discourse—but only in that relation. It cannot usefully be torn from its only proper context.

It is very important to spell out this point more precisely; and this can best be done, not by invoking such names as Wittgenstein and Barth, but by referring to recent developments in the study of religion.

At the beginning of this century anthropologists used to work by gathering reports of strange customs and beliefs collected from every corner of the earth, and classifying this material under such headings as 'totemism' or 'witchcraft'. When they came to write their books they would use these headings as a framework. Thus a chapter on witchcraft might begin with a general definition, and go on to present an astonishing cross-cultural catalogue of curiosities. Having thus set up his problem, the author would formulate a general theory of how men came to believe and to do such very odd things.

But after the First World War Malinowski and others pioneered new methods of intensive fieldwork. A classic of this kind was E. E. Evans-Pritchard's *Witchcraft, Oracles and Magic among the Azande* (1937), based on several years' close study of one people. He showed that witchcraft beliefs and practices which seem bizarre when cited at random and out of context, when studied systematically in a particular society are found to make up a coherent and (in its own terms) reasonable system. They provided, he found, an effective way of explaining and combating the varieties of human misfortune. In every culture an ordinary man may ask about his trouble, 'Why has this happened to me, and what can I do about it?'; and the Zande answer to this question is as systematic and efficacious, in its own way, as most of the others one might cite.

Here then was a remarkable *tour de force*, which has had a great influence on the study of religion. It has come to be thought (not without the help of firm guidance from the great man himself) that the search for universal definitions, and universal genetic explanations, of religious phenomena was largely wasted effort. A term like 'magic' may be kept for convenience, but we should not suppose that it has a single universal meaning. Magical beliefs and practices are different in different societies, and each one must be explained in terms of its own setting-in-life. The emphasis should be placed not so much on cross-cultural universals, but more upon the distinctiveness and the coherence of each particular cultural system.

If we relate this change of emphasis to the problem of belief in God, the implications are both positivistic and relativistic.

They are positivistic in that the old 'comparative method' of cross-cultural generalization and philosophical speculation has been rejected. We are more likely instead to hear it said that belief in God can only be accurately discussed with reference to a specific case, where what counts as God, as belief, and as the criterion of right belief have had assigned to them the definite values proper to them in a particular community. The Muslim, for example, is not talking about God in a general philosophical way, but about the-God-whose-prophet-is-Muhammad, the One God whose revelation of his will is embodied in Islamic religious Law. That is, by 'God' the Muslim means the One who is known and served only through the study of a certain sacred book, and certain practices in the way of prayers, fasts, almsgiving, pilgrimages, and so on. He does *not* suppose that true belief in Allah, the one True God, is abstractible from this very detailed context. The context is essential. Thus if we want to raise the question of an explanation and justification of his belief in God, the method of Evans-Pritchard seems to be truer to the facts than the method of a philosopher.

But the implications of this are also relativistic, because there is evidently a variety of forms of belief in a variety of specifications of God, and each particular form of theism is autonomous, emphatically proclaiming its own completeness and sole authority, and putting up a vigorous resistance to any philosopher's attempt to subsume it under, and evaluate it from the point of view of, some allegedly more universal standpoint.

We may try to overcome the difficulty here by saying that, even if there is not identity, there is surely at least an analogy between the way in which the-God-whose-prophet-is-Muhammad is the fundamental theme of Muslim religion, and the way the-God-who-is-the-Father-of-Jesus-Christ is the fundamental theme of Christian religion. Admittedly the working out, in terms of social life and institutions, of the fundamental idea is different in the two cases, but the core is surely the same?

But I doubt if the philosopher can easily secure his *locus standi* along these lines. For let us consider the familiar parallel with the rules of games. We may claim that there is an analogy between the respective roles of the king in chess, the wicket in cricket, and the goal in hockey; for in each case the strategy of the game revolves around defending your own and attacking your opponent's. But the intergame analogy, though it might be used in the very first stages of instructing a beginner, will not take anyone very far. The only way to learn chess is to learn chess-language, and the only way in which the role of the king in chess can be *precisely* specified is in the technical language of chess. There is no very useful sense in which the king, the goal, and the wicket are 'really' the same thing, and nobody learns to play games by first learning a general philosophical theory of the nature of all games. He goes straight to the particular case.

Suppose that, in spite of all this carping, a philosopher obstinately persists in proving the existence of God. To do it he must establish his premises, his method of argument, and his definition of God. But these specifications, in so far as they are truly philosophical, cannot be identical with those of any particular religion. So if he succeeds he will have created a philosophical theology like that of Descartes, or that of Aristotle: he will have created just one more theistic system which *must* be different in kind from that of any religion.

All this shows how pluralistic our approach to the study of religion is becoming. It seems that 'God' can no more have a definite universal meaning than 'witchcraft'. 'God' exists, not as a universal essence, but only in his various particular specifications, whether religious or metaphysical. We cannot speak about God absolutely, but only about 'the-God-whose-prophet-is-Muhammad', 'the God of Descartes', and so on. Nor can we argue about God absolutely, for forms of argument presuppose logical principles, which in turn are valid or invalid relative to metaphysical frameworks. If we argue within a theistic framework we will arrive at the God presupposed by that framework; and if we don't, we won't.

Before long we shall, I believe, see critics relating the classical arguments for the existence of God to the cultural contexts in which they were formulated. Thus, St Anselm's *Ontological Argument* needs to be set against the background of neoplatonic metaphysics, the social prestige of monastic life, and the monk's pursuit of the vision of God. The contemplative life was accepted as the highest conceivable life, and its Object as the greatest possible object of aspiration. Anselm's proof of God no more needed empirical premises than his way of life needed worldly justification.

St Thomas Aquinas, on the other hand, was not a monk but a friar, concerned about the social order. The *Cosmological Arguments* in his first three 'ways' are Aristotelean in terminology. He lived in a graded society in which everybody was empowered by the person next above him, and every dependent, from serf to Pope, was ultimately empowered by the one and only utterly independent Being, God, the First Cause of all. The whole social order, in ecclesiastical theory at least, hung upon God in exactly the way that is formalized in Aquinas's arguments. Again, the *Argument from Design*, in the form popular in the eighteenth century, springs from a world in which everyone who knows what craftsmanship is can recognize it in Nature without the need of an authoritative revelation or a professional priesthood to guide him. And the nineteenth-century's *Moral Argument* relates to the golden age of free enterprise and bourgeois moralism. Deeper analysis has compelled men to separate the realms of nature and morality, but God is still experienced as the Power who incites the energetic individual to discipline his own nature and to impose order upon external nature.

And the *relativism* of our own age is no less politically conditioned. The sheer size of modern societies, their internal diversity, and their enrichment by the immigration of men of very varied religious allegiances, has created a political need for a formula of concord. If a committee is drawing up a syllabus for the religious education of children in a city where people of many religions have to live together, it can scarcely avoid working on the relativistic principles I have been outlining.

But if these principles are sound, the scope for philosophical theology is very limited indeed. It will have to be conceded that in each religion God is specified in a distinctive way, and the most that can be done in the way of justifying religious doctrines is the sort of thing that Evans-Pritchard did for the Zande belief in witchcraft.

Some philosophers of religion, and some theologians, seem to be willing to accept this situation. At least religious beliefs are no longer dismissed as meaningless. It has been shown that they are fundamental structural features of whole ways of life: and that the only justification of which they are capable is one which shows in detail how they are bound up with the ways of life they generate. This is all that can be done, and it is sufficient. Moreover, the relativistic view of religion that I have been describing is not only widely held in the academic world, but is also socially necessary if we are to accept and respect religious diversity in an open society.

Nevertheless, in spite of all this, I am dissatisfied and propose to continue with the argument. Something more is needed if our original task, of justifying belief in God, is to be considered accomplished. All we have established so far is that contemporary religious thought is relativistic; and this 'sympathetic relativism', as I have called it, must be, if not our conclusion, at least the basis of our further enquiries.

RELATIVISM

Religious relativism is but one aspect of a wider issue. It was once thought, especially in Britain, that our knowledge is acquired passively. Incoming experience is imprinted upon our minds as upon blank paper, and somehow organizes itself into a system in accordance with psychological laws. But this theory is untenable. The truth is that we actively put a construction upon all our experience. The popular model which nowadays guides empirical research is that of a computer which has been programmed to search for certain patterns in its input. So I propose to call the whole system of basic concepts, models, and principles, with which we address ourselves to the world, interpret it, and shape our action within it, a 'programme'. Kant attempted, in the Critical Philosophy, to prove one programme as necessary *a priori*; but, more recently, empirical cross-cultural studies have suggested that there is a diversity of possible programmes. Relativism, then, is the doctrine that all knowledge is programmatic; that there is a diversity of possible programmes; and that there is no absolute programme in the cognitive world any more than, after Einstein, there is an absolute standpoint in the physical world. What is more, all knowledge, all argument, and even all logical principles are intra-programmatic.

Now a programme is a complete world-view, an action-guiding belief-system by which a community lives. And the world appears to be such that it can bear a variety of programmatic constructions. Groups with very different ideologies or belief-systems can flourish, and each be persuaded that the world confirms their view of it. I use the phrase 'the interpretative plasticity of the world' for this phenomenon.

A full realization of the world's interpretative plasticity is fairly recent, for it presupposes an appreciation of the historical and the cross-cultural, the diachronic and the synchronic, variegation of human consciousness such as we have only acquired in modern times. In the older European thought, both Greek and Christian, the world was usually regarded as a fully constituted system with a relatively stable and determinate structure. Now the picture is changing. The world-order is not fully determinate in such a way that the human mind has nothing more to do than to accommodate itself to a structure already laid down before men came on the scene. Rather, the determination of the world's structure is completed only by human thought and action. A plastic world interacts with a human conceptual framework to gain a finished shape. But there is no one finished shape. Instead, there are a variety of possible constructions of reality. The history of thought in a particular culture is the history of an ongoing interaction between men's changing interpretative frameworks and the various world-pictures which those frameworks yield as they are applied to experience. The mind which scans the world, and the meanings which the world so scanned delivers up to the mind, are both constantly evolving in tandem.

Yet our very ability thus to formulate the problem of relativism is also the clue to our ability to transcend it. For there is an obvious incoherence in the thoroughgoing relativist doctrine, namely that if it is applied to itself a paradox results. For if the proposition that 'every item of our knowledge is relative to an interpretative framework' is known to be true, non-relativistically, then it is itself an exception to the rule it states: but if it is itself true only relativistically, then it might be untrue in another perspective. The fact is that if men can become conscious of their own fundamental categories of thought, and if they are capable of intellectual and moral *innovation*, then they are not the prisoners of their own programmes. R. G. Collingwood, in his *Essay on Metaphysics* (1940), failed to discuss how conceptual change is possible: but it is possible, because it occurs; and therefore he was wrong to speak of our 'absolute presuppositions' as unquestionable.

Conceptual change occurs, and therefore men have the mental capacity for it. I call that capacity 'spirituality'. By 'spirituality' I mean our reflexive ability to transcend ourselves by becoming aware of and by being able to criticize and even change our own fundamental patterns of thought. We are spirit in so far as we can *change our minds*, in the strongest sense of that phrase. There have been periods in European history when several basic world-pictures have co-existed in competition; the seventeenth century was one. In such a period there is a more-than-ordinary sense of spiritual excitement. But the ability to change one's mind is present always, and in everyone: it is manifest in *humour*, as when one must transcend oneself spiritually in order to see that the joke is on oneself; it is manifest in *repentance*, when one both affirms and transcends the self that one has been hitherto; it is manifest in *iconoclasm*, when someone overthrows socially accepted religious symbols; and it is manifest in *conversion* of every kind.

Our ability, then, to transcend ourselves in freedom is what marks us as spirit. But we cannot think of ourselves as pure spirit. The self as spirit is known only as the condition of the possibility of fundamental moral and intellectual change. Unable to conceive ourselves as pure spirit, we have to return to the empirical self, which is always found incarnated in a particular cognitive framework. The self as pure spirit is no more capturable in thought than a trans-linguistic moment can be captured as we translate a piece of prose into another language. There are only the two different pieces of language: the hinge between them must be supposed, but cannot itself be seized in language.

SPIRIT

Now in all this we are running very close to what we were saying earlier about religion. A great religious tradition is clearly a highly complex programme through which and by which a community lives. This programme is often called the 'Law' of that religion. It includes sacred writings, institutions, and rituals; it includes historical traditions, doctrinal and moral teachings, and exemplary stories; it includes forms of symbolic representation, modes of prayer, and so on: the whole being distinctive of a particular community. The entire religious system or programme is claimed to be an authoritative representation of the supreme object of faith and so an authoritative guide towards the attainment of that object. He who lives by this programme and is steeped in it is living the good life because he is rightly oriented towards the supreme object of faith.

It was in this sense that we were saying earlier that a Muslim believer does not believe in a metaphysical, trans-religious God. He believes in Allah-whose-prophet-is-Muhammad; that is, his perception of the world, his thought of God, and his direction of his life, are governed by the whole system called Islam in and by which he lives. The system is an integral whole which specifies for him what 'God' is.

Is 'God', then, purely intra-programmatic? No, because the religious system *both* asserts the authoritativeness of its own particular programme, *and* asserts that God transcends the programme. The crucial analogy is this: *as the self as spirit is to the programme-bound empirical self, so God as spirit is to the programmatic God of the religious system*. The self is the fundamental analogy of God.

A religious group which is stagnating, living in relative isolation and feeling no need, or having no opportunity, to take seriously the views of other groups may perhaps never feel forced to make this all-important distinction. God-in-symbolic-representation, the programmatic God, is taken to be God simply. Such a state of affairs has been called 'henotheism', or more strongly, 'idolatry', and in my terminology, the God of such a religion is not apprehended as spirit. And where God is not spirit, man cannot be so either. But a great religious tradition affirms both the authoritativeness *and the relativity* of its own programme, and so makes the transition from a closed and tribal to an open, universal, and spiritual faith. Peaceful encounter with other peoples, through trade, is often the key. In the Hebrew Bible, it is reflection on the religious status of foreign nations which makes possible the emergence of a spiritual monotheism; and in Greece philosophical theism emerged from a background of religious pluralism.

The crucial distinction, then, is that between God-in-the-programme, the God of practical, institutional religion, on the one hand; and the God who is pure transcendent spirit on the other. If, in a religion, the negative way has precedence over the affirmative way, if the possibility of a mystical transcendence of programmatic religion is kept in view, and if a legitimate possibility of iconoclasm is retained, then that religion is spiritual. As Pascal said, 'God being hidden, any religion that does not declare him to be hidden is not true'; and conversely, so long as religion does affirm its own relativity, it remains alive in spirit. God absolute, God as pure spirit, can be expressed only by insisting upon the relativity of even the most comprehensive and powerful religious programme; an affirmation which alone can make a religion spiritually liberating, as opposed to spiritually imprisoning.

In Christianity the analogy between God and the self is particularly ingeniously brought out by the canonization of both the Old and New Testaments. God himself is said to switch the programme from one structure of representations (in its time authoritative) to another. This entrenchment of the principle of relativity in the transition from the Old to the New Dispensation has given Christianity its historical momentum and capacity for spiritual renewal. But the same principle is apparent elsewhere, and indeed the analogy between the way the self is conceived and the way ultimate reality is conceived is universal. And if, as I have argued, we must conceive the self as capable of transcending the culturally-determined programmes through which it ordinarily apprehends the world, then we must correspondingly conceive God as pure unknowable spirit who transcends the culturally determined symbolic apparatus through which he is ordinarily apprehended. The way we conceive the self obliges us to be monotheists.

For the old doctrine that God made man in his own image is true as a mythical *résumé* of the history of consciousness. God was spirit before men were spirit. Those old rebels, from Elijah to Luther, from Socrates to Kant, were our forefathers. They transcended the prevailing programmatic representations of God, and so became spirit themselves, by their denunciation of idolatry and their witness to a God who was pure spirit. Divine spirituality made humanly possible.

SPIRIT AND LETTER

We can now complete our argument by sketching some elements of the phenomenology of spirit.

In the first place, it is clear that there are two quite different kinds of atheism, both of which are wrong. One claims that man cannot exist as spirit at all, and seeks to imprison him within a single cultural programme or conceptual apparatus. It does this for political reasons: the idea of spirit is feared as politically subversive, for it suggests that no collective belief-system whatever can be absolute; at some point or other it can be and must be transcended in freedom. Thus the thought that the single man can be spirit, that he is capable of radical innovation, is repugnant and threatening to totalitarians of every kind, because it implies that no social system or ideology can be secured for ever against change. I am certainly not thinking only of 'scientific socialism' here: the Harvard psychologist B. F. Skinner, in his book *Beyond Freedom and Dignity*, quite expressly argues that society can no longer afford to believe in individual freedom, and his views were endorsed by the American Humanist Association: an outstanding example of *trahison des clercs*. But this sort of atheism is not only morally repugnant; it is, as I have argued, simply false.

The second form of atheism to be rejected is the Romantic view that man can exist alone as pure spirit. It emerged among the left wing of the Hegelians, becoming in the nineteenth century the creed of Bohemian artists, and in the twentieth century almost a popular orthodoxy. Since Feuerbach and Max Stirner the atheistic philosophy of spirit has often allowed the truth of my claim that the Divine Spirit is the historical progenitor of the human spirit: it agrees, that is, that man first became spirit by thinking of God as spirit. But the Divine Spirit is nothing but a projected expression of the human spirit, striving to come to birth. When at last God becomes man, man becomes God and 'everything is permitted'. Man can live alone as spirit. His capacity for self-transcendence and pure innovation is self-created and requires no other grounding. Since the self as pure spirit is unknowable, and abstracted from all specific cognitive or moral determinations, it can only be conceived as pure anarchic creative energy, which exults in its own capacity impartially to create and destroy every possible programme. So the Bohemian artist and the anarchist were permitted and indeed called to be universal rebels, and to overthrow every sort of artistic and social convention. We have seen, first in the artistic *avant-garde* and then in social life, the confusion, the pessimism, and the nihilism which have resulted.

It is a novel objection to atheism that it is not universalizable; but it is clearly true of this kind of atheism. It is logically unable to be a basis for social life. As an exceptional protest against an oppressively complacent bourgeois culture, the extreme individualism of Stirner and his more recent fellow-travellers makes sense; but as a mass phenomenon in its own right it is clearly absurd, for it must in principle refuse to evolve any communal artistic, moral, or cognitive programme.

So there are two sorts of atheism. One says that the individual man can exist alone as pure spirit; and it must lead to anarchy, for its exaltation of the free individual spirit is incompatible with the claims of social life. The other denies that man can be spirit at all; and it infallibly produces social tyranny. Between the two, a theistic philosophy of spirit alone can rightly balance the claims of society and of freedom. For it both sustains social life by proclaiming the authority and the sufficiency of a particular programme, and also witnesses to the possibility of transcending it. It gives reasons for loyalty to a culture, a publicly established programme, and it leaves a place for spirituality. And it unites men in spirit, rather than divides them, for God as universal unknowable spirit is a *common* focus for the spiritual aspirations of all men.

There are two ways to God: the affirmative way, which goes through the programme; and the negative way, which transcends it.

The affirmative way proclaims the sufficiency for salvation of a 'revealed' system of symbolic representations of the divine. God is represented and dealt with in human terms, in ways that engage the affections and the imagination, and can bind together a society of living men. Admittedly God-as-represented-in-the-programme is not God absolutely, but only a symbolic representation of God. But it is nevertheless declared to be an *authoritative* representation, which does not seriously mislead men and is sufficient.

The negative way to God proclaims that in his own transcendent spirituality God altogether surpasses any programmatic representation of him. The movement of the mind to God must be by an inner abnegation, a stripping away of imagery, and so a movement towards unknowing. When the self has reached complete detachment it no longer knows itself, and when it has renounced all symbolic representations of God it no longer knows God. A self that no longer knows itself communes in darkness with a God no longer known.

Early Buddhism may be the purest expression of the negative way, but belief in God returns to the programme and accepts the world. Or rather, it exists in a movement between these poles, of projection and cancellation, speech and silence, expression and recollection, community and solitude. A justification of belief in God ought to be true to the nature of belief in God; and that is why my attempted justification has taken the strange form it has.

The religious group I belong to has a reputation for loving the middle way, and for having perpetrated some pretty tenuous lines of argument in its time. But has anyone before ever commended theism as a middle way between two sorts of atheism?

We have not yet given any reason for linking belief in God as transcendent spirit with one religious programme rather than another, so I must draw some final conclusions on that point.

Since the self as pure spirit, and God as pure spirit, are entirely trans-programmatic (or, in the usual terminology, transcendent), they are beyond the scope of metaphysics. The self as pure spirit is the condition of the possibility of freedom and innovation; God as pure spirit is the condition of the possibility of the fellowship of spirits. As the self as pure spirit transcends in freedom the various world-pictures *it* creates, so God as pure spirit transcends in freedom the actual world, which *he* creates. But there is no common metaphysical doctrine underlying all the various theistic faiths, and religion cannot be transcended philosophically. Nor is any natural theology possible. The most that can be said is that the principal world religions bear witness to the limits of thought, to their own relativity, and so to the transcendent. So there is only the transcendent, and the various positive religious programmes that witness to it. Why then choose one rather than another? I accept the one which, as it seems to me, embodies the idea of spirit in its central myths more perfectly than any other, namely Christianity. God represents himself to men in human form: but in that form he must die, and we with him. The revelation of God in Christ, and yet the necessity for the death of Christ, epitomizes the ideas I have been clumsily expounding, and has inspired them.

10

On the Finality of Christ

Except in the Moslem world, and in the most populous parts of Asia, Christianity has become in modern times the principal religious faith of mankind. The revival and expansion of the Roman Catholic Church since the middle of the nineteenth century have been especially remarkable. The process of decolonization has not in any way reduced the power and attractiveness of European culture. Even China, although in one of its xenophobic phases, remains under the sway of a European political ideology, and European science and technology.

Yet there is a paradox in all this. For as European culture has become global, Europe itself has declined in power and confidence; as Roman Catholicism has flourished and spread under the inspiration of ultramontanism, it has come to experience a crisis of authority; and as the influence of Christ and the Christian movement have become world-wide, many Christians have come to doubt the absoluteness of Christianity and the finality of Christ. It has become conventional in the so-called 'Western' countries to deplore the cultural and the religious imperialism of our nineteenth-century forebears, while yet in many respects the triumphal progress of Western-style industrialization, of socialism, and of Christian expansion still continues. Christian doubts about the finality of Christ are surely part of the wider paradox of the European *daimon*. We colonized Africa, but we could not help sowing in it the political and moral ideas which would in time enable it to rise up and expel us. We went out as missionaries of Christ, but we also could not but encourage the peoples we encountered to rediscover and reaffirm their own ancient faiths against ours. Forced to concede moral and political parity in the one case, we are now increasingly inclined to accord them religious parity in the other.

It is against this background that we can best see how traditional Christianity developed its understanding of the finality of Christ, and why it has run into difficulties in modern times.

I

No reader of the New Testament can fail to observe that its most fundamental affirmation concerns the uniqueness, the sole sufficiency, and the finality of what God has done in Jesus Christ. This conviction is expressed in various ways, and it is not altogether easy to clarify and define it, but of its presence there can be no doubt. That Jesus is God's only Son; that only through him can men be saved; that God acted in him once and for all; that world history will be wound up by him; and that he is God's chief executive, seated henceforth at God's right hand: these are some of the forms in which it is expressed. The events described in the Gospels are unique and unrepeatable. What is happening here is such as has never happened before, and can never happen again. It is quite compatible with Buddhism, indeed it is held by Buddhists, that the state of Enlightenment attained by the Buddha under the Bo-tree may be independently reached by other men before and since: whereas Christianity regards the life, death, and resurrection of Christ as in some way essentially unique and unrepeatable. But already we are in need of more precise statement, for surely Jesus himself said that the rejection, persecution, execution, and vindication of a righteous man is something that has all too often happened before, and will often happen again? The pattern of his ministry, suffering, death, and resurrection is, he declares, amply foreshadowed in old tradition and will be re-enacted, both in ritual and life, in the future. So what is unique about this particular enactment of the pattern? The answer seems to be that all the earlier enactments were anticipations of it, and all the later ones will take place in the power of it. That is to say, the special and unique status of the Christ-event is relative to a theology of history.

For the Jews, like other peoples, divided time into great epochs, which were differentiated theologically. What makes Christ final is that he winds up one epoch and initiates a new one, whose character will be determined by him. Thus the idea of a change of dispensation, the end of an old order and the beginning of a new, is needed in order to explain the finality of Christ.

But we still do not have enough, for according to the Bible there had been such changes of dispensation before. One was marked by the eating of the forbidden fruit and man's expulsion from Paradise; another by the Flood and the Bow in the Cloud; another by Abram's leaving Ur and his arrival in Canaan; and another by the Exodus and the giving of the Law on Mount Sinai. If the age of Moses had been ended by Christ, why should not Christ in turn similarly give place to another? The answer, of course, is that the age Christ inaugurates is the Last Age. He cannot be superseded, for his age is necessarily final, and so he is final.

We notice here that if Christians seriously embrace the idea of a post-Christian era, they must on this account abandon the finality of Christ: and indeed must cease to be Christians in the sense normal hitherto.

So far then we have established that Christ's finality and absoluteness were explained by reference to an eschatological scheme, and a Jewish one at that. But if so, is not the message about Jesus strictly relative to Jewish religion and tradition? How can it be intelligible outside that context? In the earliest Church the decision to take the Gospel to the gentile world was reached only with difficulty. At any rate it was necessary, if you were to become a Christian, to accept the Jewish theology of history, and every Christian must become a kind of spiritual Jew before he could grasp the place of Christ in God's unfolding plan for mankind. The Hebrew Bible, or the Septuagint, must be canonized. To appreciate the finality of the New Dispensation you must first accept, and see yourself as having in some way been involved in, the Old.

Still more important, you must accept the Jews' own estimate of their own central place in universal history, as a light to the gentiles, the trunk of the human tree, and the people whose history is of universal significance.

Until as recently as the seventeenth century this worked remarkably well. The Bible is, after all, a very wide-ranging book. It knows Africa, Asia and Europe, and the civilizations of Mesopotamia, Egypt, Greece and Rome. It knows tribal, agricultural and urban society. Until the seventeenth century all Christian men, wherever they lived, saw universal history, and their own spiritual pedigree, as running back through Rome, Greece, Israel, Egypt, and on to Mesopotamia. Jews spread alongside Christians; and it is worth remembering, alongside the tragedy of that relationship, that the Jews were in a strange way necessary to Christians, as living monuments to the Christian view of the past. The Old Testament was the chief source-book for the early chapters of universal history, and there was no very significant conflict between the Christian understanding of the past and the best available secular evidence. In such a context the idea of the finality of Christ fitted surprisingly well. The basic distinction in world-history was that between A.D. and B.C. In the years before Christ men lived under the Law: those were the years of the slave-societies of remote antiquity. In the years of Grace men had come to mature freedom in Christ. Now the world was hastening to its end. For until the end of the seventeenth century time past and time future were both thought of as finite. The history of man reached back to the beginning of the world, which indeed had been made for no other purpose than the acting-out of the drama of salvation. There had been about 4000 years before Christ, and there would be 1000 (as was at first thought) or perhaps 2000 years after him. Thus the drama was now in its last act; and we are reminded that not only was world history finite, but its whole course was seen as analogous to the course of a human life, and the Bible was a literary expression of the whole of it.

So the finality of Christ was understood at first in relation to Jewish eschatological ideas. When the Christian faith moved into the Greco-Roman world it successfully assimilated the culture it found. From Irenaeus to Milton the Christian world-view was a remarkably vigorous and successful elaboration of the Jewish sacred history, giving a comprehensive and impressively accurate historical–theological pedigree to all the known civilized world. The finality of Christ was preached in relation to this entire system.

And this is why we began with the paradox of Christianity's simultaneous expansion and loss of confidence. Since Milton's time the unity of Christian culture has been broken up by a huge enlargement of our perspectives in several dimensions at once. In the days of Leibniz and Newton the doctrine of progress appeared, with the denial of the finitude of future history, and so by implication of the finality of Christ. Even before then the voyages of exploration had made it plain that there were many human societies beyond the reach of any plausible extension of the usual historical–theological framework. What was the relation of the God of Christendom to Japan, or to the American peoples? Since Mark Twain jeered at it as 'chloroform in print', the Book of Mormon has been more laughed at than read. But it bravely sets out to answer an important question: What is the place of the New World in God's plan of salvation? It gives the New World a sacred pedigree parallel to the Old World's, and cross-linked with it. Similar attempts are still being made on behalf of the Far East. If we think them absurd, then it is clear that we no longer believe that our religious and cultural pedigree is coextensive with the entire race, but rather recognize that it is only one of several such pedigrees.

A compromise has been suggested, among others by Dr Raymond Pannikar in *The Unknown Christ of Hinduism* (London, 1965), to the effect that since Christ is universal he finalizes not just one, but every great religious tradition. He is the fulfilment of the aspirations of India as much as of Israel. It is unrealistic and unnecessary to require Indians to renounce their own religious heritage and adopt the Hebrew Bible as their only way to Christ. In Europe the New Testament is prefixed by the Hebrew Bible. But in India it would surely be appropriate to preface the New Testament with Indian sacred books such as the Upaniṣads. To Christianize India is not to persuade her to disclaim her heritage, but rather to show Christ as its fulfilment.

One appreciates the cultural pressures which have given rise to this suggestion; pressures felt in a very acute form by Arab Christians in the Middle East today. But there are difficulties. How can the finality of Christ be proclaimed except in relation to the Jewish idea of history? Where time is cyclical there can be no *unrepeatable* incarnation: and unless God is orchestrating the historical process towards a climax there can be no place for a *final* incarnation. The doctrine of the finality of Christ is inescapably bound up with a view of time peculiar to the Jews, and so the New Testament cannot be separated from the Old.

The importance of the idea of time was realized in an amusing way by an obscure theologian called John Craig. He followed Locke in accepting the view that the credibility of testimony decays with the passage of time; and so, in a book published in 1699, argued that the historical facts of Jesus's life must cease to be believed by the year A.D. 3150.[1] Craig concluded that Christ must return by then, but what is really striking about his argument is that, for the first time I think, a theologian has seen the problem of relating the finality of Christ to a possibly indefinite futurity here on earth.

There have been other similar enlargements of perspective. As long ago as 1600 it was possible to speculate that the universe might contain other inhabited worlds than our own. Was the Christian revelation for them also, or did it relate to this world only?

Again, during the eighteenth century men were becoming

[1] John Hunt, *Religious Thought in England*, vol. III (London, 1873), p. 124.

accustomed to the idea that the world might be everlasting in past time, as well as in future time. The curtain may have been raised for countless ages before any human actors appeared. The word *aeon*, which in the Bible means a period of around 1,000 years, is now used by scientists to denote a period of one thousand million years.

So the idea that the Old Testament was the trunk of the tree of universal history was already in some difficulty in the eighteenth century, when a still more serious development took place, in the growing dissociation of theology from history. David Hume and others wrote history in a new detached spirit which seemed surprisingly free from any ideological or moral patterning. The new critical history began to demythologize the past, to deprive it of its power to shape a world-view and guide life, and so undermined not merely the Christian but any and every religious or mythical picture of the sacred past. Soon Lessing was to ask his famous question, How can necessary truths of reason be derived from contingent historical facts? If history contains nothing but finely judged probabilities, if everything in history is relative, then we can never justifiably claim to have discerned the absolute and the certain in history. There can never be historical evidence sufficient to prove that a man's death in Palestine is of eternal significance to me today. I may lean on Church history and say that the meaning of that man's death is so deeply a part of our cultural history that we must all come to terms with it. The psychologist C. G. Jung would have said that much. But such an argument does not even pretend to be applicable to a Buddhist monk in Sri Lanka.

II

So much, then, for the classical Christian way of explaining belief in the finality of Christ, by embedding it in a panoramic theology of history. One leading theologian of today, Wolfhart Pannenberg, has attempted to revive the idea of a Christian understanding of universal history. How successful he will be only time can tell, but the intellectual difficulties are by now formidable. What other possibilities are there?

The principal one, also rooted in the New Testament, explains the finality of Christ by relating it to a theological anthropology or (in a more modern idiom) an existential analysis of the human condition. The aim is to establish certain universal generalizations about all men who ever have lived or will live. These statements are of somewhat uncertain status. They touch upon the fields of metaphysics, ethics, and psychology. Sometimes they seem to be necessary truths to which there can be no exceptions, and sometimes they seem to be empirical generalizations, confirmed or otherwise in our daily experience. Their status is something of a problem: but every culture and religion makes such statements, for there is always some implicit or explicit model of man; so let us not trouble ourselves further about their status, but simply recite them, as follows: Man is a rational creature, made by God and for God, the supreme end of whose existence is to know and enjoy God eternally. Now, to know God one must please him, and to please him one must be righteous and do the works of righteousness. But though man has some knowledge of what righteousness is— enough to know he lacks it—he lacks the power to do it. He is in the predicament known as the bondage of the will. He knows what is the road to lasting happiness, but cannot make any progress along it. His despair and need of a saviour are total: he needs one who can effect a total transformation of the self in him. For him, when he discovers Christ to be such a saviour, that saviour is final; for the saviour does nothing less than re-create him, rescuing him from utter damnation for eternal happiness.

The great Protestant anthropologies, from Luther to Ritschl, Bultmann, and Tillich, explain the finality of Christ in terms of the desperate predicament from which he rescues the believer, and the total re-creation of the self which he brings about. To enforce the point a whole series of extreme assertions is produced. Man prior to justification is wholly wicked, his will utterly in bondage, and he is therefore shut off from God and the hope of heaven. He can do nothing to save himself, for he is corrupt through and through. No non-Christian can be saved, or please God in any way at all.

The Protestant anthropology, and the psychological and moral outlook created by it, have been deeply influential but are now of course almost totally rejected by all modern men. And indeed it is open to very damaging criticisms. The extreme dualism implied in the doctrines of sin and redemption is not easy to reconcile with the universalism implied in the Christian doctrine of creation. There will be a suspicion that the diagnosis of the disease has been framed in such terms as to make it evident that only Christ can be the remedy. Indeed, this is true historically, for early Christianity consciously set up a complex parallel between Adam, the prototype of fallen man, and Christ, the prototype of redeemed man; and some theologians, such as Karl Barth, have in any case quite openly derived their account of man's disease from their account of God's remedy for it. What is more, how can the universality and objectivity of the Christian doctrine of fallen man be proved to men outside the Christian tradition, when the claims are no longer made that we are all descended from an original pair, that the Fall was an historical event, and that the effects of the Fall are transmitted to all their descendants? To men outside the Christian tradition it will surely seem that the Protestant anthropology is not an absolute diagnosis of the universal human condition but a cultural product, intelligible in one cultural setting but irrelevant in another.

Doctrines are of course not only descriptive but prescriptive. They *recommend* a certain perspective. Perhaps the Protestant anthropology is not purporting to be an accurate analysis of how an Indian sees his own situation before God, but is rather a *recommendation* to adopt a certain self-understanding? In that case it must presumably be tested ethically: and so it becomes vulnerable to the severe moral criticisms that have so often been levelled against it, and which, to my mind, are conclusive.

III

The classical Christian account of the finality of Christ set it in the context of a great theological account of universal history. Christ was final because the Christian era was the Last Age of the world. The typical Protestant explanation of the finality of Christ grounded it upon the experience of redemption from a state of utter despair and damnation. The doctrine of man showed him to be trapped and lost without Christ, freed and saved in Christ.

We have found reason to be dissatisfied with both these accounts; but, in any case, it may well be retorted that we have so far begged the most important question of all. Christ is final, not just because of the part he is found to play in the drama of cosmic redemption, or individual redemption, but because of his own unique relation to God.

For, according to Christianity, Jesus Christ is the only-begotten Son of God, incarnate once for all in human form. It is not that Jesus's status depends upon the role he plays in the redemption drama, but that because he is God Incarnate the redemption drama unfolds around him. The fundamental idea is that there has been a unique embodiment of God in that short stretch of past history which was the life of Jesus. Starting from this conviction a theological picture of the world, or of the human heart, prior to his coming, and a theological picture at the new situation which the Incarnation creates, can both be constructed. At any rate, the Incarnation is the fundamental idea, and it is in some degree independent of the two themes we have hitherto discussed: for one *could* hold that there has been an unrepeatable embodiment of God in Jesus of Nazareth, without being committed to any one particular apocalyptic or dispensational view of history, or any particular view of man fallen and redeemed. And if Jesus's status is thus independent, it can be reaffirmed outside its original apocalyptic context.

However, a belief in the Incarnation which is not set in *any* context is empty. Some reasons have to be given for believing it, and its religious implications have to be spelt out in some way. If the doctrine of the Incarnation be maintained in a very strong form, the case might be made somewhat as follows:

There has been a once-for-all inhistorization (to use H. H. Farmer's term[2]) of God in Jesus of Nazareth. This event is unique, and above reason. Given the modern understanding of the nature of historical knowledge, its occurrence admittedly cannot be proved by historical method alone. To take an obvious example, the sinlessness of Christ can scarcely be proved from the modest, and controversial, evidence we have for the life of Jesus. But the Incarnation is at least *consonant* with the recorded evidence as to Jesus's character, teaching, miracles, and resurrection, and the long tradition of Christian faith. All these strands of evidence point to a mystery which they cannot *compel* us, but may well *lead* us, to acknowledge.

Furthermore, if God has embodied himself absolutely in a particular life, then this event will leave a historical residue behind it. It will leave mementos. So a strong doctrine of the Incarnation, as many Catholic theologians have rightly claimed, becomes the base upon which a whole series of subsequent doctrines are piled: the physical resurrection of Christ, his real presence in the Eucharist, the infallibility of the Church which witnesses to him, and so on —the whole edifice, in fact, of feudal or 'christendom' Christianity. An absolute incarnation of God in time means that there can be a visible absolute authority in matters of faith and morals. Here we

[2] *Revelation and Religion* (London, 1954), pp. 195-6.

have, I believe, the central theme of the neo-mediaeval and authoritarian forms of Christianity which flourished between the mid-nineteenth and mid-twentieth centuries, and which had a powerful appeal to men whose souls craved dogmatic certainty. It is the sudden failure of confidence in this kind of Christianity which has so unnerved people in recent years.

Yet there were obvious objections to this very positive and strong form of incarnation doctrine. Its demand for unconditional commitment and submission to authority has exposed it to increasing moral criticism, and given rise to a well-founded suspicion that its intellectual bases are not very strong. Its insistence that the man Jesus of Nazareth is an absolute image of God in human form is not consistent, as Jews and Moslems are well aware, with classical monotheism. The eternal God, and a historical man, are two beings of quite different ontological status. It is simply unintelligible to declare them identical. What is more, the humanism of our age, which guides us in our reading of the Gospels, shows us in them a quite different figure from the Jesus of the high incarnationalists. According to the high incarnationalists, Jesus claimed to be God. Yet when we read the Gospels Jesus appears as one who prays to God, whose relation to God is one of faith, not identity, and who repeatedly denies that he in any sense 'is' God.[3] He suffers, he is tempted, he experiences storms of anger, exultant triumph, despair, compassion, and joy. He is not at all like a stately immobile icon of God. He does not appear as one who *embodies* God, but as one who with the whole of his passionate nature witnesses *to* God.

So the strong incarnationalist doctrine, that Jesus of Nazareth is an absolute icon of God, looks very implausible now. It developed at the moment when the old Christologies of Jesus as the Word of God, or as the Spirit-filled Man of God, were replaced by the new Christology of Jesus as God's only-begotten Son. And this happened just in time for Constantine. A father and his son are two beings of the same kind, and the son can indeed be a second edition, a replica of his father: whereas a man and his utterance are two things of *different* kinds. A Christology of Jesus as the Word of God is obviously, from a theological point of view, much less misleading than a Christology of Jesus as God's only son. But feudal Christianity needed a Son of God to validate the whole structure of society. A high incarnational Christianity says the things feudalism

---

[3] E.g. Mark 10.18, Luke 12.14, Mark 13.32, etc.

wants to hear; that man was created for serfdom, and that there is a historical absolute to which he must wholly submit himself. No doubt many Christians today will find all this offensive, but I fear it is uncomfortably close to the truth; and it explains why modern political upheavals, and above all the cry for liberation, have created a historical situation in which high incarnationalist Christianity cannot be defended successfully.

It is a strange and sad paradox, that the Protestant anthropology should in practice so often create an inner, psychological deformation and tyranny, and that the doctrine of the Incarnation should so readily lend itself to the establishment of an external and objective tyranny. Christ came to set men free, but modern man, who certainly longs for freedom, sees in the usual Christian accounts of Christ only forms and sources of enslavement. It is, perhaps, this realization that has set so many searching for a new kind of Christology, free from the moral ambiguities which have disfigured the older kinds. It is a reminder to us, in our present inquiry, of the dangers which beset any attempt to articulate the finality of Christ.

IV

So we turn at last to my constructive proposal, which seeks to steer a midcourse between the pure religious relativism which says that every major religion is an equally valid way to God, and the absolutist language in which traditional Christian faith has so often been expressed.

My argument is that we should think of Christ, not in terms of Son and Image, but in such terms as *Word* and *Witness*. Theology says there cannot be any wholly adequate temporal image of the eternal and invisible God, and history says that nothing historical can be absolute and certain. Morality says that an absolute historical incarnation of God must generate a reactionary and tyrannical social order. So for me, Jesus's finality lies not in himself but (as he himself says) in what he proclaims, and in the way he bears witness to it. Jesus is final, not as an absolute icon of God—there cannot be such a thing—but because of the way he bears witness to what is final and unsurpassable. His finality is relative to man's spiritual aspirations. In the ages before him, the *summum bonum*, the highest good, was for the few. If it had ever been attained by man at all, it had been attained only by an élite company of godlike men—

great kings, chiefs, heroes, prophets, and holy men. The mass of men were destined for the underworld, or trapped on the wheel of rebirth. It was not for them to scale heaven. The Gods were jealous of their privileges, and admitted few to share them. The *summum bonum* might perhaps be attained by the masses; but then, only by the last generations, as in modern socialism, those who had died before being simply lost. There is no harrowing of hell in Marxism. But for Jesus every single human being is directly summoned to attain the highest good here and now, in the kingdom of God. When that has been preached, no further spiritual development can take us beyond it. A limit has been reached.

And Jesus's life is a final paradigm of man's relation to God, for he dramatically exemplifies the triumph and tragedy of faith: the triumph of rapturous communion with God in the assurance of God's love for men; and the tragedy of our relation to God, that we must nevertheless die and be utterly bereft of all that we have known of God and believed about him. He experienced the yes and the no of faith, the affirmation and the rejection of images, in a definitive way. To an icon-christology this is a scandal: but to me it is central.

Jesus's ethical teaching is final, in the sense that there can be no higher moral value than utter purity of heart, disinterestedness, and commitment to the way of love. There is not, and there cannot be, any higher moral value than this: again, it is ultimate, and cannot be superseded.

And Jesus's spirituality is final, in the sense that he all the time affirms, and yet in affirming transcends, the thought-situation in which he is set. An icon-christology cannot understand, and indeed usually ignores, the ever-present note of mocking irony in every recorded utterance of Jesus. Yet his irony is the clue to the understanding of Jesus, for it is his way of evoking the sense of the presence of God. He forces upon us a critical and questing spirit of restless dissatisfaction with all mundane values, institutions, and achievements, and a longing for that absolute good which we shall have to die to attain. It is, above all, through his ironical spirituality that he has imprinted his own distinctive vision upon mankind, and planted a seed of saving self-doubt in his Church. Christianity must never be allowed to become a mere religion, a positive symbolic system built around the idea of the incarnation. For it is infinitely more than that. It is a religion and a critique of religion, a religion which speaks of God by negating itself, which affirms a man who teasingly denied himself. Unfortunately the term 'antichrist' has already been pre-empted for another purpose: but Jesus is in truth both Messiah and antimessiah; for he never merely fulfils our aspirations, but invariably confounds them too: and it is in that ironical dialectic that he conveys his message.

The point of view I have outlined is based firmly on the Gospels, and the tradition of Jesus's own sayings as they have always been heard in the Church, and as they still stand in the light of modern biblical criticism. I affirm the finality of Christ in the sense that there can be no superseding of the central themes to which Jesus bears witness, nor any nobler way than his of bearing witness to them—the way of death. To claim iconic absoluteness for Jesus would subvert his message: how could men iconize an iconoclast without being aware of the absurd irony of their own mistake? But the finality I attribute to Jesus is not in any sense exclusive. Claims to exclusive finality have all too often been heard in Christianity, but any idea of exclusive property in divine truth is itself a manifestly ironical mistake.

11

On Christian Existence in a Pluralist Society

Suppose there is someone who, in the late twentieth century, in the urban industrial society of 'the West', wants to live a Christian life; or, more simply, wants to know what a Christian life in such an environment would be, so that he can make up his mind whether to try to live it or not; then what shall we say to him? What kind of life would a Christian life be today?

The first and most obvious reply is to take up a New Testament and say, 'If you read this book and ruminate upon it, you will see that it recommends certain attitudes, character-traits, and values. Though there are admittedly incoherencies and difficulties within the book, and although the social context from which the book arose is very different from today's, nevertheless the imaginative and attentive reader is given a clear enough picture of what kind of person he ought to strive to be if he wishes to be a Christian. Take this line from St Paul: "The harvest of the Spirit is love, joy, peace, patience, kindness, goodness, fidelity, gentleness, and self-control" (Galatians 5.22, *NEB*); or again, "Be generous to one another, tender-hearted, forgiving one another as God in Christ forgave you" (Ephesians 4.32). There is surely nothing obscure here. The fact that we live in a world of television sets and aeroplanes makes not the slightest difference to the intelligibility of the moral ideal here set before us. A Christian life is simply a life which exhibits the virtues listed here.'

This statement is admirably straightforward, and I do not intend to dispute it, so far as it goes. I only want to say that it is a less conclusive and adequate answer to our opening question than at first appears. It concentrates attention on the personal qualities of the individual, but it does not say anything about his relation to the social setting in which he lives and which—whatever his personal qualities may or may not be—very largely determines the shape of his day-to-day life. It is when we ask *this* question, about the relation of Christianity to its cultural context, that difficulties arise.

Let us suppose then that we are comparing our hypothetical Christian with another hypothetical figure, the ordinary upright citizen, the naturally good man. How should the Christian's life differ from his?

The first answer goes like this. The Christian does much the same things in much the same way as any other good citizen, but does them Christianly, and does a few specifically Christian things as well. These extra things are traditionally summarized under the heads of prayer, fasting, and almsgiving. The Christian, that is, performs the extra religious duties of attending public worship and generally being a practising churchman; he orders his life ascetically by observing customs such as saying grace before meals, or giving up things for Lent; and he is active in some way in voluntary or charitable work.

Many people, however, are critical of this description of the Christian life. It presupposes that there exists, apart from Christianity, a social order and public value-system which, so far as it goes, is good and compatible with Christianity. So, if a man is a good citizen in the world's eyes, all he need do to become a Christian is to 'top up' his life with a specifically religious supplementary ingredient, and the two elements will blend smoothly together to produce a unified whole, the Christian life. But is it true that the ordinary British way of life, lived out through the various social roles of worker, householder, and so on, embodies and expresses an agreed standard of natural goodness which is a sweet and fertile soil for the Spirit to work in and produce a rich crop of Christian virtues? Perhaps being conformed to this world, far from being a satisfactory foundation for the Christian life, cuts one off from it entirely.

So the second answer, aiming for unity and for purity of heart, says that the Christian admittedly does much the same things as his neighbour, and to the carnal eye seems to do them in much the same way. But there is a secret difference. He pecks his wife, strides down the street, sits in the train, steps into the office, and deals with his mail; but all the time he refers everything to the eternal. He *seems* to live the same life as the next man, but inwardly by faith he relates every moment of life to eternity and so lives in eternal life. His life is a continuous invisible transformation of experience into eternity. Only in the most extreme situations, such as most people never encounter, will he become manifestly different from the next man.

Such a view of Christian ethics, one may surmise, might be taken by a Lutheran who had studied Kant; and so it was. It has been expressed with supreme eloquence in some of the writings of Sören Kierkegaard. But he came to reject it. It is the ethics of a spy, a man who lives a double life, a man whose inner reality is concealed behind his outer behaviour. But the Christian life cannot be a double life, and the process of redemption cannot be for ever invisible, if the Redeemer is the Creator. Inner and outer lives must be unified.

So the third answer must be that the Christian seeks to live in a manner entirely determined by and expressive of his Christian faith. The classical procedure is to read the Sermon on the Mount with close attention, decide what it says, and then sally forth and act accordingly. It is true that not many people have actually carried out such a programme, but at any rate those few who have certainly attracted attention and made a mark upon the world. Perhaps nothing less has the right to be called a Christian life.

But even this answer is not without difficulties. It calls for a certain bloody-minded indifference to ordinary social claims. St Francis went so far as to disown his father publicly, stripping himself naked and handing back his clothes. Leo Tolstoy became enraptured with the Sermon on the Mount, but did not leave home. Instead he became a very great and good man who was at the same time an intolerable old ogre who made his family's life wretched: a not uncommon phenomenon.

So these three answers to the problems of Christian ethics are none of them without difficulties. Again, to recapitulate what we have said so far, it seems beyond doubt that the New Testament does recommend a definite cluster of character-traits, which hang together well. We can tell pretty clearly what the Christian *character* is, and I for one judge it admirable. The real problem is that of the relation of the Christian life to the cultural setting in which it is lived. A. N. Whitehead said that Christianity is a religion in search of a metaphysic. We may widen his observation and say that Christianity is a religion ill at ease in time, always restless; seeking embodiment in a social order, but never able to settle down in any particular culture. Christendom has never been as clear-cut and stable a thing as Islam. There has always been difficulty in making a good translation of the original rapturous vision into durable social institutions. Every renewal in Christianity has gone through the series of stages that we can discern in the New Testament itself.

The starting-point is a moment of pure originality, which utterly forgets the claims of the past and the anxieties of the future. The saint is rapt out of time, absorbed in the holiness and the love of God. His whole being is pure adoration. There is only one possible way of life for him, that of a wandering ecstatic preacher. He is delighted to have nowhere to lay his head, for he rests all the time in the bosom of God. His joy and his liberty bring him followers, and more followers. They will include women and children, and people with responsibilities. There will be converts who need to be trained. As the community grows there will be a demand for organization—some source of food, somewhere to sleep, a more settled life. It will be held, at first, that the common vision has, of itself, the power to create a sufficient degree of organization, beginning with a kind of primitive communism. But as the community grows a need is felt for leaders, rank, ritual, procedures for admission and expulsion, and so on. Soon some members will be evidently part-timers, who continue to earn a living and fulfil their external social duties, while in addition devoting their leisure time to the life of the new community. They will need training and advice as to how they can spiritually reconcile the two realms between which their lives have become divided.

And by now we have arrived, already, at my three interpretations of Christian ethics. To take an analogy from the hippies in modern times, there is the original San Francisco full-time drop-out; there is the part-time hippy, who works in an office from Monday to Friday and puts on hippy gear at weekends; and there is the spiritual hippy, outwardly fully secularized, but striving inwardly to live his worldly life in a genuinely hippy spirit. To take the Franciscan example, there is the original purity of life of Francis and Brother Bernard, his first companion; there is the settled life of later conventual friars with an income and a roof over their heads; and there is, perhaps, the devout lay tertiary who tries as hard as he can the most difficult trick of all, to live an entirely secular life in an entirely Franciscan spirit.

So far we have explained our problem, but we have made no progress towards solving it. To do that, we must make a detour. I want to consider some different kinds of relation of religion to society.

Let us begin with small-scale, preliterate, tribal society; with, if you like, 'primitive' society. In this kind of society there is no distinction between religion and culture. Indeed. there are few clear distinctions of any kind. The self, society, and the cosmos (which includes the gods) are not clearly distinguished from each other. The personal and the impersonal are not clearly distinguished; and neither are the claims of the gods and the authority of society. Human consciousness, and human thought come to expression not, as with us, in the inner life and beliefs of individuals, but in a collective way, in social structures and socially generated myths. There is little awareness of the varieties of human character, of the inner life of individuals, or of individual moral or intellectual freedom. The leading virtues are virtues like piety and honour: loyalty to social structures, and respect for social roles. The capital sins are sins like impiety and disrespect: disloyalty to society and reluctance to accept one's allotted place in it. The self, in fact, is passive and dormant, radically subordinated to social structures. The tribe is a complete universe, which knows no other. There is only one way to make a bow, to be a warrior or a wife, to kill a pig, to build a house, and to bury the dead. The gods, nature, society, and duty are all bound together in one. In our exhaustingly complicated world we may well look back nostalgically at such societies, with their harmony, their contentedness, their splendid art, and their ritualized emotion.

But of course we could not possibly live in such a society, and there cannot be belief in a transcendent God in such a society. The self is not yet sufficiently developed for the term 'belief' to be applicable.

The development of mankind out of tribal society is a very laborious business. It is not just a matter of cities and writing. Soon after men moved over to a settled agricultural life, cities began to develop. In the cities astronomy and number began. They were needed because the king and the farmer needed a calendar for agriculture and measures of time for social administration; and everybody needed measures of quantity in order to organize the gathering, exchange, and distribution of produce and goods. But all this could happen—as in pre-Columbian America—while society remained basically tribal and the self still undifferentiated.

The crucial thing is not so much civilization as trade: the non-hostile encounter of different tribal universes. Trade requires the learning of a foreign language, and therefore the entry into another world-view. This, and this alone, forces the clarification of human thought. Aware of other peoples, we now have to distinguish *our* world from *the* world, society from nature. Slowly and painfully, we begin to distinguish society from the cosmos, the individual from society, and God from the cosmos.

One book tells almost the whole story of the education of the human race. It starts with a nomadic, tribal society; it moves on to a confederation of tribes; they settle and become an agricultural people, and become aware of other gods and other ways of life; they develop a feudal monarchy and begin to deal with other nations; brilliant individuals arise who can distinguish God's authority from that of the king and of society, and so think of God's relation to other peoples; the feudal monarchy is destroyed, and the surviving people have all of them to confront the intellectual problem of living under alien gods in an alien culture. Out of this situation arises a new religion, with clearer ideas of God, the world, society and the self than ever before. The individual transcends his social and natural setting as God transcends the world: from now each individual is unique, and has his own unique relation to God. The book is, of course, the Old Testament, and its people that most urban, most quick-witted and highly-conscious of human groups, the Jews.

The change in morality which these developments brought about can be illustrated by one or two examples. About 975 BC one of King David's sons, Amnon, was attracted to his half-sister Tamar. He feigned illness and asked that she should nurse him. David authorized this, and Tamar prepared some food and took it into the sickroom. There Amnon seized her and made his intentions all too plain. Tamar expressed her sense of moral outrage by saying, 'Such a thing is not done in Israel!' Morality is still tribal: it is not yet a matter of individual conscience, but of social practice.

Yet, only a few centuries later the moral atmosphere begins to change radically. The done thing, the majority practice, what has always been done, is no longer a sufficient guide to conduct. God begins to be interested, not so much in the group collectively as in individuals. He looks to see, not whether you have kept the rules, but whether your heart is pure. The law of right conduct will no longer be mediated through king, temple, priest, prophet and wise man, but will well up in the heart of each righteous man.

As the self emerges into consciousness of its own freedom and uniqueness the idea of society and the idea of God change. Sociologists, who have an ugly word for everything, call the process one of 'privatization', and often talk as if it is something that has been happening only since the Reformation, or since the Industrial Revolution. But really the Old Testament is about it.

We can therefore envisage a spectrum of different relationships between religion, and society. At one end, in primitive society, religion and morality are wholly public, and the self barely exists. Concepts such as 'freedom', 'conscience', and 'faith' simply have not yet arisen.

At the other extreme, in a highly pluralistic society, religion and morality are almost entirely private. Objective institutions and rules are disparaged. There is a great emphasis on self-awareness, on the private realm, on religious liberty and liberty of conscience. The main virtues are authenticity and spontaneity. The sins are hypocrisy and acceptance of social constraints. It is a world in which everybody almost makes up his own religion, and scorns acquiescence in social norms or collective beliefs.

In the primitive world social stability is the chief good, and all life is public. The self as free spirit is as yet unknown. At the opposite extreme, in liberal pluralistic society, the self affirms itself so successfully that social structures, a common morality, and a common world-picture are overthrown, and society seems on the verge of disintegration.

Christianity was born into a relatively pluralistic world, the late Hellenistic period, and from the first it converted individuals and baptized them one by one. It stressed the voluntary character of faith, and freedom of conscience. It was willing to criticize, and in certain respects to repudiate, the structures of the society, or societies, in which it lived. Thus early Christian religion, especially while the Church as an institution was still relatively undeveloped, leaned towards the private rather than the public end of our spectrum.

But by the fifth century things were slipping fast the other way. In his extraordinarily vivid and powerful self-awareness Augustine stands out in a period when the general movement of history and of Christianity is towards the publicization of religion and the regression of the self into dormancy. I hope we see now why it is that the more deeply a society is Christianized the less Christian (in another sense) it becomes. The self falls asleep, as faith and morals become more collective and less individual, and Christendom loses its divine restlessness and power of self-criticism.

The change I am describing can also be seen as a change from urban to rural or pagan religion. Christianity was at first urban. Urban man is more self-aware, and urban religion is more private, more conscious, more mobile, more emotional, and more critical.

Rural or pagan religion, by contrast, is more deeply embedded in social structures, more tenacious and less conscious. New religious movements can only begin in an urban setting, for only urban religion has the critical self-awareness that makes innovation thinkable.

It follows from all this that we should be wary of idealizing the rural Christendom of the past: the kind of Christian society which, after a fashion, still exists in the most backward areas of Western and Eastern Europe. It was very beautiful and tranquil; but Christianity had become so deeply engrained in the rhythms of social life that it became unconscious, and so uncritical. Russian orthodoxy was a conspicuous example. In one sense the Russian Orthodox Church was one of the most beautiful religious institutions there has ever been, and it did profoundly Christianize the life of the Russian peasant. Yet, at another level, it could be said to have been a failure, for that same profound sacralization of life kept the Christian self in a kind of enchanted sleep, in which it could not sufficiently question the justice of social order, or even clearly distinguish the claims of God, of the Church, and of the Tsar from each other.

These considerations cast a new light on the much-discussed problem of secularization. The usual picture represents the old sacralized social order of Christendom decaying in recent centuries, and this process of decline is called secularization. But our reflections have led us in the direction of a much more complicated picture. Jewish and early Christian consciousness was strongly urban, mobile and self-aware. Christendom was a kind of paganized form of Christianity, an enchanted sleep. Belief in God demands a kind of critical self-awareness which ought to prevent Christianity from ever becoming deeply embedded in any social order. God's relation to the world is mirrored in self-awareness, in the way in which the free critical spirit of conscience stands above and judges the empirical, socially determined self. The man of faith has no continuing city here below: he is *meant* to be mobile, *in via*. Thus, at least since the fourteenth century, new movements in Christianity have been urban and individualistic in spirit. The urban Christian radical has been trying to reawaken Christianity from the sleep of Christendom. He has stressed faith rather than ritual, self-awareness rather than social order. It is true that, to a sociologist's eye, the cities look dechristianized in modern times. Broadly speaking, the further you get from London, the more people go to church. But it is also true that new religious movements still do, and can only, begin in cities and that in urban culture the Christian is more highly conscious of himself, his faith, and his mission.

The point here is similar to one which psychologists make about anxiety. Anxiety, restlessness, is life itself: a life unspurred by anxiety would be torpid and ineffectual. Similarly, the Christian's relation to his social environment must always have a flavour of restlessness and dissatisfaction. True Christianity is, after all, more urban than rural in spirit. It does not simply accept the social order, nor does it expect ever to be able completely to reconcile Christianity and social life in this world. The pillar of fire moves on; there is no resting place here, for the Christian's citizenship is in Heaven.

So at last we reach our title, Christian existence in a pluralist society. Yes, our society is pluralist in that it is overwhelmingly urban, and, even more than the cities of antiquity, full of jostling philosophies. It is a ferment of different world-views, conflicting diagnoses of and remedies for the human condition. It is rapidly changing, swept by emotional storms, restless, self-aware, and oscillating between optimism and pessimism about the future. All this is true, and yet our argument suggests that precisely because of all this it is a favourable rather than an unfavourable environment for the Christian life. Our contemporaries, and we ourselves, often dream of an older and simpler order of things, a small-scale society in which religion and morality are built-in, taken for granted, and not worried about; a social order which will *give* us our beliefs, and *tell* us our rights and duties. We dream, in a word, of retiring to the country. But it is only a dream, and even if we could realize it, we should lose a great deal more than we should gain. For when Christian belief and morality become objectified in the social order, the self falls asleep, and Christianity falls asleep. The movement of European culture away from a rural and sacralized Christendom to an urban and pluralistic society may be described as a process of secularization, but it can also be described as forcing a reawakening of Christianity.

So, when we talked about three possible interpretations of Christian ethics—the life-styles, roughly speaking, of the bourgeois Christian, of the early Kierkegaard, and of St Francis—we were asking the wrong questions about them. For we supposed, *a priori*, that a harmonious relationship between Christianity and social life must be possible, that the Christian life ought to be unified and more or less tranquil. As so many writers have done, we set up that straw man, the ordinary upright citizen, and then tried to depict the Christian's life in relation to his. Starting from the life of an ordinary upright citizen, the Christian life could be portrayed as a *supplemented* version of his life (bourgeois Christianity), a *transformed* version of it (Kierkegaard), or a radical alternative to it (Francis). But the conclusions we have been led to are that the ordinary upright citizen is himself, in urban, pluralist society, a problematic character: and that the Christian has no reason to *expect* to live a unified life in harmony with his cultural environment. On the contrary, a measure of internal tension and stress is the price of spiritual life.

People sometimes complain that since the French Revolution the intelligentsia have been in a condition of continuous disaffection and alienation, and that modern culture is predominantly critical rather than constructive, concerned to undermine rather than to affirm the established order of things. Well, all that may be true; but if so, it is part of a movement brought into the world by Jews and Christians. The only alternative to it nowadays is totalitarianism, the creeping totalitarianism of technology and benevolent social planning; and even totalitarianism cannot survive for long in the modern world, because the kind of self-awareness which Christian and Jewish faith brought into the world will not tolerate it. In the future we shall have more, not less, of the pluralistic, urban, and highly self-aware kind of society that has been growing up around us.

What then will Christian existence be like in a world in which the 'privatization' of belief has been carried further than ever?

It will be diverse. Our argument suggests that it is neither practicable nor desirable to try to entrench Christianity in social structures in the future, in the way that was attempted in the past. No nostalgia, then, for Christendom. That kind of social embodiment of religion was never an entirely satisfactory expression of Christianity, for it reconciled faith and society at an unconscious and basically sub-Christian level. It sought a degree of standardization in doctrine, morality and ritual which the New Testament, at least, does not exhibit or require, and for which the individual had to pay a heavy price.

We need to try to reconcile the individual with the community at a higher level than has yet been achieved. There is common ground: the particular kind of self-awareness that the relation to God creates; the longing for perfection expressed in the Sermon

on the Mount; the struggle to reconcile the claims of social justice
and of the spiritual life; and the traditional Christian virtues—in
a word, the spirit of Christ. There is material here upon the basis
of which Christians can establish a common universe of discourse
about morality and spiritual life. That common universe *is* the
Church. There *can* be a Church in an age of pluralism and individualism.

And we need not be afraid of irrationalism. The old monolithic
societies *looked* more rational, but only because in them one belief-
system and ethic was objectified in the social structure. The terms
of public debate were very narrow. In our kind of society there is
a breadth of public discussion and disagreement, and daily encounter with a vast diversity of information and opinion, such as
men a few centuries ago could not have dreamed of. It was
easy to be rational then, in relation to a much simpler culture.
But we should not give way to the fear that religion and morality
are doomed to be subjective and arbitrary now. Not so. It is harder
to be rational now, but our range of possible debate and experiment
and communication with each other is far wider than it was, and
that is a great gain.

Index